Called
to be
God's People

by
Robert Street

The International Spiritual Life Commission

Its report, implications and challenges

INTERNATIONAL HEADQUARTERS
101 Queen Victoria Street, London EC4P 4EP

Copyright © 1999 The General of The Salvation Army
First published by International Headquarters 1999
This edition reprinted by UK Territory 2001
ISBN 0 85412 689 9

Robert Street, who served as Chairman of the International
Spiritual Life Commission, became a Salvation Army officer
in 1969. In addition to commanding corps in the UK, he has
been Editor of *The War Cry*, Editor-in-Chief, and Divisional
Commander for Anglia. His commitment to the wider Church
found expression in his chairmanship of Norfolk Churches
Together and Suffolk Churches Together. Lieut-Colonel Street
is currently Principal of the William Booth College, London.
He is married to Lieut-Colonel Janet Street and has three
children.

Printed by Halstan & Co. Ltd., Amersham, Bucks., England

Contents

The Questions and Scripture printed in the previously published pamphlet *Called to be God's People* are presented at the conclusion of each of the chapters which deal with a specific Call. The *New International Version* is used unless otherwise stated.

Foreword

by General Paul A. Rader

The report of the International Spiritual Life Commission has now been received around the Army world. It has been published in a variety of formats in order to make it as accessible as possible to Salvationists and those who desire to understand us better. We are encouraged to learn that it is being discussed widely and vigorously and that its compelling call to be God's people is being heard sensitively.

In order to facilitate understanding of its vital themes and the theological and practical reflection that underlies its emphases, the Chairman of the Commission, Lieut-Colonel Robert Street, has prepared this insightful and well-written commentary on the report. The chapters will not only afford a clearer understanding of the implications of the Calls but also stimulate further discussion and action.

Nothing is more critical for our future effectiveness in mission as we move into the new millennium than our inner strength as a Movement. Nothing is of higher priority than the nurturing of our inner life, growing in grace and understanding, in holiness of heart and life, and in our experience of the risen life of Christ, present among us, experienced by us, and expressed through us in the quality of our lives and service.

I warmly commend this helpful volume and urge its widest possible use as corps fellowships begin to explore together the full promise of our freedom in Christ in response to the call to be God's people, moving forward in freedom to embrace God's future.

Introduction

In March 1996, General Paul A. Rader appointed an International Spiritual Life Commission to review the ways in which The Salvation Army cultivates and sustains the spiritual life of its people. Following discussions at the International Conference of Leaders, held in Hong Kong in 1994, he decided that the time had arrived for an in-depth re-examination of public and private expressions of worship and faith. With The Salvation Army having moved into more than 100 countries, some ongoing clarification and re-emphasis of those aspects and practices which are integral to the Army's spiritual life were seen to be vital to the unity, progress and health of the Movement.

Speaking to members of the International Spiritual Life Commission when they met for their first meeting in July 1996, the General explained: 'In recent years, and for a variety of reasons, we have begun to come more to terms with our churchly identity – that is, the accepted and publicly-acknowledged fact that we are the church home for something upwards of two million people in the world. For most of them we are their primary, if not only, point of insertion into the body of Christ. We are the fellowship within which they experience their connectedness with the body of Christ.

'It is the Army through its corps life that provides them with essential instruction in Christian doctrine and an understanding truth of Scripture. It is the Army that provides the primary setting for worship for most of our people. What they know of worship, they know from their experience in the Army. What they know of prayer, they have learned at the Army. What they know of personal spiritual discipline, they learned from us. It is through the Army they experience their relationship to the broader Christian community and establish their identity within that community as *bona fide* Christian believers.

'Simply put, it is time for us to take more seriously issues related to our inner life. We owe it to our people. It is essential to maintaining the engine of commitment and passion. Our mission is energised by our spirituality.

'Further, the Evangelical Church, and the Army within it, is more embattled by powerful spiritual forces than ever before. Our people need to be armoured against the enemy of their souls.

'The proliferation of false ideologies and religious options, and the far greater ease of access to these options in a pluralistic climate of growing fascination with varieties of religious experiences and systems, requires that our own people have a clearer grasp of their own faith and the capacity to support it through the word of God.

'The complexity of moral and ethical issues in these times requires more thorough instruction in the implications of Christian discipleship in today's world and an ability to apply the truth of Scripture to contemporary ethical concerns.

'We have a responsibility to ensure that we are not denying our people necessary means of grace and that their participation in the life of the Army through their corps affords them every available advantage in living the Christian life.'

In effect, the Army must acknowledge that, as it has been energised by God the Holy Spirit to establish its work and ministry throughout the world, it has become 'a people of God'. In his First Epistle, the apostle Peter tells the Christians of his day: 'Once you were not a people, but now you are the people of God' (2:10). In the middle of the 19th century The Salvation Army didn't exist. It was not part of the Church of God. Now it is. By God's directing, its people have become a people within the people of God. The cultivating and sustaining of the spiritual life of this people are paramount.

Initially, 15 members of the International Spiritual Life Commission came together for that first meeting under the chairmanship of Commissioner Ian Cutmore. (Commissioner Cutmore was unable to continue the chairmanship after the first meeting.) The number of members later increased by three, and some of the 10 corresponding members were involved in subsequent meetings. Each meeting lasted for five days and there were five of them. They took place during July and November 1996, and in March, July and September/October 1997. Each meeting was held in London and hosted at either the International College for Officers, the William Booth Memorial Training College or Sunbury Court.

The first week had the effect of opening members' eyes to the hopes, aspirations, needs and priorities of one another and the territories from which each person had travelled. In addition, members often had a wider knowledge of the Army and the world than only their present situation. Officers of all ranks were included, as were three non-officers. One of these, Susan Harris, a young Salvationist from Coventry City Corps, UK Territory, joined the Commission following a request from the International Youth Forum (held in Southern Africa) for a more youthful input.

As the Commission met to begin its deliberations it was apparent that all members were aware of the enormity of the task and of their own sense of inadequacy. Nevertheless, each person brought personal convictions and it was important that these were shared. As the sharing began it became obvious that 'easy solutions' would not be possible and a great deal of listening to one another was both desirable and essential. The priorities of Sweden, for instance, were not the priorities of Brazil. The concerns of Zimbabwe were not the major concerns of India. A decision which might enhance ministry in one country could even harm the effectiveness of ministry in another.

The issues to come under discussion demanded integrity from those who considered them. They were as follows:

The study of the word of God. This included the teaching ministry of corps through regular prayer meetings, educational programmes and small groups.

The prayer life of the Army. This included the manner in which encouragement is given for the enhancement of prayer through corporate worship, small groups and devotional exercises.

Public worship. This was to be re-examined as a means of grace and spiritual growth.

Salvation Army ceremonies. The significance of this subject became more apparent as other topics were addressed.

The place of the mercy seat.

The place of retreats, conferences, special meetings, spiritual direction and mentoring.

The place of other traditional spiritual disciplines. These were to include fasting, silence, meditation, solitude and simplicity.

The Salvation Army's approach to the sacramental dimension of life was also to be included in the review. The significance of the absence of the Sacraments in their traditional form in Army worship (especially baptism and Holy Communion) was to be assessed, acknowledging that these sacraments had not been part of Army practice for more than 100 years. Was there a case for their introduction or re-introduction? (Holy Communion was practised in the Army's earliest days.)

It was always the General's intention that any Salvationist should feel able to contribute to the Commission. Each territory was asked to identify people who would keep in contact with the Commission, and forward papers and requests for further consideration. Many Salvationists – officers, soldiers, adherents and friends – made direct contact through the Commission's secretary (initially Lieut-Colonel John Major and then Lieut-Colonel Earl Robinson) and this resulted in members needing to set aside time at the beginning of each meeting to catch up on masses of correspondence. Consideration was given to all correspondence, as spiritual convictions and hopes were expressed in various ways. Not surprisingly, contrasting opinions received by the Commission were always in evidence, so the need to ensure a balanced discussion on each subject was vital.

The fact that Commission members themselves held different views on some subjects was not a problem. It was essential and welcomed. The members knew they were required to make joint recommendations, publish findings and present a way forward for the Army, so a sense of united purpose in the diversity of opinion was vital. The need for unity within the Holy Spirit was acknowledged throughout all discussions, deliberations, prayers and decision-making, and proved to be not only a real blessing to the members but also a special confirmation on the Commission's efforts.

It is hoped that *Called to be God's People* will challenge Salvationists everywhere to make their spiritual life all God intends it to be. The initial report, with the Calls and affirmations, is presented in this book, as is some of the thinking behind the Calls. Statements regarding the Army's position on the sacraments of Holy Communion and baptism are presented too. They explain concisely what is at the heart of the Army's thinking on these matters – matters which have brought controversy as well as blessing within the Church for centuries.

The impossibility of sharing all that was said or considered must be acknowledged from the start. Parts of papers and presentations are shared, but sometimes without reference to source. To ensure acknowledgement every time would not make for easy reading, nor would it take into account the development of thought that occurred through open discussion. It is sufficient to acknowledge that Commission members each had a part to play in pointing the Army towards the things which they believe God wants it to embrace and then put into action by his Spirit.

The chapters which deal with specific Calls conclude with questions which are also found in the booklet of the same name, *Called to be God's People*. The booklet has been produced for corps groups. It recognises that the Calls will only be effective when they are embraced at corps level, according to the situation, need and culture of each corps. Put simply, every corps has its own thinking, praying and living-out to do.

The Commission has presented the Calls. Its members must now join their fellow-Salvationists at the grass roots in looking at what God wills for his people. As we are called to be God's people, let us ensure we *are* God's people.

Forward in Freedom!
The Chairman's Report: First presented to the International Conference of Leaders in Melbourne, March 1998

The Salvation Army has a God-given freedom in Christ which, if used to the full, could enrich the Army's spiritual life and total ministry in ways far beyond those already enjoyed.

This freedom should never be underestimated, undervalued or neglected but be warmly embraced and positively engaged to the glory of God and for the extension of his Kingdom. It is firmly rooted in the Army's tradition, has always been at the heart of its most inspiring and effective initiatives, and points the way ahead for what God has planned for his people.

This is the conviction of the International Spiritual Life Commission, convened by the General to examine and identify aspects of the Army's life which are essential or integral to the spiritual growth of individual Salvationists and the Movement itself.

In its five week-long meetings the Commission became increasingly aware both of the rich cultural diversity possessed by the Army in the 104 countries in which it is working, and of the unifying power found in its shared universal beliefs and practices.

The Commission also took note of the correspondence, papers, suggestions and support given by fellow-Salvationists who took up the worldwide opportunity to share in this challenging and exciting task.

Among aspects Salvationists confirmed as integral to the Army's life were its ministry to the unchurched, the priesthood of all believers (total mobilisation), personal salvation, holiness of life, the use of the mercy seat, and social ministry (unreservedly given).

It was when giving consideration to practices of other churches that the value of the Army's freedom in Christ was particularly evident. The setting of fixed forms of words or acts is not part of Salvationist tradition, though the value placed upon them by some other denominations is recognised.

A great deal of time, prayer and consultation was given to examining the value of introducing or reintroducing a form of Holy Communion. In addition to considering the large amount of correspondence on the subject, the Commission held a number of Bible studies, gave time to further prayer and also arranged for the visit of a former chairman of the Church of England's Doctrine Commission. Many points of view of various persuasions and convictions were considered, and the membership of the Commission itself helpfully reflected those differences. Although some differences still exist, the Commission has been able to present its recommendations in a spirit of unity and harmony, recognising the vast potential for innovative worship and ministry within the freedom which the Army already enjoys in Christ.

It was recognised that the forms of worship used by Christians of the Early Church (including the common meal) were not known as *sacraments*, yet the importance of keeping Christ's atoning sacrifice at the centre of its corporate worship has always been vital to the spiritual life of the Army. Recognising the freedom to celebrate Christ's real presence at all meals and in all meetings, the Commission's statement on Holy Communion encourages Salvationists to use the opportunity to explore together the significance of the simple meals shared by Jesus and his friends, and by the first Christians. It also encourages the development of resources for such events, which would vary according to culture, without ritualising particular words or actions.

The Army's long-held beliefs that no particular outward observance is necessary to inward grace, and that God's grace is freely and readily accessible to all people at all times and in all places, were unanimously reaffirmed, as was every Salvationist's freedom to share in communion services conducted in other Christian gatherings.

When considering the subject of baptism the Commission recognised the scriptural truth that 'there is one body and one Spirit . . .one Lord, one faith, one baptism; one God and Father of all, who is over all and through all and in all' (Ephesians 4:5-6) and that 'all who are in Christ are baptised into the one body by the Holy Spirit' (1 Corinthians 12:13).

There are many ways in which Christians publicly witness to having been baptised into Christ's body. Water baptism is one of them, but the ceremony, like that of the swearing-in of a Salvation Army soldier, is essentially a witness to the life-changing encounter with Christ which has already happened. The ceremony itself is not the encounter and should not be confused with the act of becoming a Christian. Bearing this in mind, the Commission recommends that the Soldier's Covenant, signed by new soldiers, should incorporate reference to each soldier's baptism into Christ by the Holy Spirit at the moment of conversion.

Specific **recommendations** made by the Commission to the General highlighted ways in which preaching and teaching of the word of God should be given prominence. They encourage cultural expressions of worship and give special emphasis to Bible study, education and training. The importance of Salvationists being better informed and more adequately educated on matters of faith was frequently highlighted in the Commission's deliberations.

There is also a strong recommendation that Army leadership at every level should conform to the biblical model of servant leadership. To assist with this, a re-evaluation of structures, ranks and systems is urged, as is the need to make spirituality an essential quality and qualification for leadership in the Movement. Training and development of officers and local officers to assist their spiritual development is also regarded as a priority.

In addition to making recommendations at the General's request for his consideration (together with the Army's international leaders), the Commission makes a **Call to Salvationists** worldwide to recognise that any outward movement of love for the world requires first of all an inward movement from each Christian towards God. 'The vitality of our spiritual life as a Movement will be seen and tested in our turning to the world in evangelism and service, but the springs of our spiritual life are to be found in our turning to God in worship, in the disciplines of life in the Spirit, and in the study of God's word,' it says. Twelve specific Calls are made, together with complementary affirmations.

In the Call the Commission expresses its belief that each Salvationist's equipping for spiritual warfare must come from God and be rooted in the conviction of the triumph of Christ. The living out of the Christian life in all its dimensions – personal, relational, social and political – can only be achieved by embracing Christ's Lordship and the Holy Spirit's enabling.

The Commission has recognised the impossibility of providing (and the foolishness of attempting to provide) guidelines and strategies that would suit all countries and cultures in which the Army operates. One of the Army's greatest strengths is its diversity of culture, methods and resources.

Nevertheless, the Commission is ready to assist with relevant resourcing by providing material that can be used for teaching, clarifying and supporting fellow-Salvationists as they respond to a new and revitalised recognition of what God can do in and through his Army, by his Spirit and in the freedom which Christ gives.

The Calls

The chapters that follow introduce the Commission's Call to Salvationists and highlight 12 vital areas of the Army's spiritual life.

Each of the 12 Calls is supplemented and amplified by an affirmation.

The Call to Salvationists

The Founders of The Salvation Army declared their belief that God raised up our Movement to enter partnership with him in his 'great business' of saving the world. We call upon Salvationists worldwide to reaffirm our shared calling to this great purpose, as signified in our name. Salvation begins with conversion to Christ, but it does not end there. The transformation of an individual leads to a transformation of relationships, of families, of communities, of nations. We long for and anticipate with joy the new creation of all things in Christ. Our mission is God's mission. God in love reaches out through his people to a suffering and needy world, a world that he loves. In mission we express in word and deed and through the totality of our lives the compassion of God for the lost.

Our identification with God in this outward movement of love for the world requires a corresponding inward movement from ourselves towards God. Christ says 'Come to me' before he says 'Go into the world'. These two movements are in relation to each other, like breathing in and breathing out. To engage in one movement to the exclusion of the other is the way of death. To engage in both is the way of life. The vitality of our spiritual life as a Movement will be seen and tested in our turning to the world in evangelism and service, but the springs of our spiritual life are to be found in our turning to God in worship, in the disciplines of life in the Spirit, and in the study of God's word.

Call to Worship

We call Salvationists worldwide to worship and proclaim the living God, and to seek in every meeting a vital encounter with the Lord of Life, using relevant cultural forms and languages.

We affirm that God invites us to a meeting in which God is present, God speaks, and God acts. In our meetings we celebrate and experience the promised presence of Christ with his people. Christ crucified, risen and glorified is the focal point, the epicentre of our worship. We offer worship to the Father, through the Son, in the Spirit, in our own words, in acts which engage our whole being: body, soul and mind. We sing the ancient song of creation to its Creator, we sing the new song of the redeemed to their Redeemer. We hear proclaimed the word of redemption, the call to mission and the promise of life in the Spirit.

A VISITOR is reported to have walked into the quietness of a Quaker meeting, turned to someone nearby and enquired, 'When does the service begin?' The answer came back, 'The service begins as soon as the meeting is over.'

Apart from illustrating that the word 'service' is used in the western world to indicate worship in a formal setting as well as practical Christian ministry, the incident in the Quaker meeting house reminds us that true worship involves more than religious observances.

Worship comes from the heart. The words spoken in a formal setting or in quietness are best matched by daily living which demonstrates all that we profess with our lips.

When members of the Commission met to discuss worship, they began their own worship with these words of Horatius Bonar:

> *Fill thou my life, O Lord my God,*
> *In every part with praise,*
> *That my whole being may proclaim*
> *Thy being and thy ways.*
> *Not for the lip of praise alone,*
> *Nor e'en the praising heart*
> *I ask, but for a life made up*
> *Of praise in every part!*

The Call to Worship is a call to 'worship and proclaim' the living God. Worship and proclamation should go hand in hand. In the words of General Frederick Coutts: 'We cannot truly worship God unless we work for him with such powers as we may possess.'

If our acts of worship are sincere, if they are genuine, our lives will naturally reveal Christ. The call to proclaim has within it a challenge to be proactive. We are to announce the lordship of Jesus. We are called to evangelise. But Christ says 'Come to me' before he says 'Go into the world'. We find the springs of our spiritual life in our turning to God in private moments of prayer and devotion, as well as in our worship together.

Our meetings are vital to the spiritual life we share. They allow for freedom and, within The Salvation Army, include prayer, praise, Scripture, songs and testimony, as well as personal preparation by the leader. They resource us for service. They have the potential to fire us for mission, to inspire us for sharing the gospel. They have the capacity to change our lives, to redirect them, all because God is in the meeting. He is present, he speaks and he acts.

Nevertheless, we acknowledge that not every meeting fulfils its purpose. There are times when we fail either to hear what God is saying or to be aware of what he is doing. The attitude we bring to a meeting dictates what we receive. The meeting is not primarily with each other, it is with God. If individually we are to benefit from the worship we offer, we must ensure the communication with God is two-way.

In Isaiah 55:3 (*GNB*) the Lord issues an invitation: 'Listen now, my people, and come to me: Come to me, and you will have life!' There is a sense of relationship in the invitation. In Matthew 11:28 Jesus is recorded as inviting his disciples to 'Come to me, all of you who are tired from carrying heavy loads, and I will give you rest.' Scripture reminds us again and again that God invites us to come to him.

The Psalms abound with calls to worship. Psalm 95:6 implores: 'Come, let us bow down and worship him: let us kneel before the Lord, our Maker!' The psalmist captures the majesty of God, and the awe and wonder of his people. He was ready for a vital encounter. He wanted to be with God, to see God, to understand God. When we come to worship, the same enthusiasm combined with the same openness will bring us close to God.

In this age, when modern miracles of technology surround us, the human sense of awe, respect and reverence are not what they once were. But if God Almighty is to make a difference in our lives, we must recognise and acknowledge his greatness. If we approach him carelessly, casually, or with such familiarity that we forget his holiness and our unworthiness, we will meet only with disappointment.

Jesus said some vital things about worship. Speaking to a Samaritan woman he pointed out: 'God is spirit, and his worshippers must worship in spirit and in truth' (John 4:24). The meeting house in which worship takes place may be either conducive or distracting to worship, the person leading the worship may be helpful or a hindrance, but much more important is how we prepare ourselves for worship and the attitude in which we come to our God.

In the past few years much has been made of differing styles of worship. Some are more visual than others, some are more expressive. Some are 'charismatic'. Some are contemplative. Some formal, some informal. For many the quieter, more reflective periods are the moments when they are closest to God. When worship is at its quietest they hear God the loudest. For others it is different – and God is more than capable of meeting our individual needs as we allow him!

11

Colonel Catherine Baird spoke of worship in this way:

Loving Friend, we stand before thee
Without merit or pretence;
Teach us, guide us as we follow,
Trusting in thy sure defence;
We would contemplate thy goodness,
Finding fortitude and grace,
Learning of our Father's mercy
In the beauty of thy face.

In its affirmation, the Commission acknowledges that 'in our meetings we celebrate and experience the promised presence of Christ with his people. Christ crucified, risen and glorified is the focal point, the epicentre of our worship.' We worship Christ. He is the reason for our meeting. He has reconciled us to God. Because of this we 'offer worship to the Father, through the Son, in the Spirit, in acts which engage our whole being: body, soul and mind'.

The Salvation Army's emphasis on the possibility of a personal relationship with Jesus Christ means that verses such as this one by Frances Ridley Havergal not only have deep meaning but also are an aid to moving forward in Christian experience:

Speak to me by name, O Master,
Let me know it is to me.
Speak, that I may follow faster,
With a step more firm and free,
Where the shepherd leads the flock
In the shadow of the rock.

When Jesus was 12 years old, his parents lost him on the way home from Jerusalem. Luke's Gospel tells us (2:44) that they thought Jesus 'was in their company', so 'they began looking for him among their relatives and friends'. Similarly, it is all too easy to arrive at a meeting expecting God to be present because he is 'in the company', among our relatives and friends. If we neglect our own commitment, our own contribution, our own relationship with Christ, the meeting will do very little for us. *With* our commitment, contribution and sense of relationship with Jesus, every meeting holds many possibilities.

Even so, we should look for Christ in each other. One of the ways in which God is present in the meeting is in the lives of the people who are there. In Matthew 18:20 Jesus promises that 'where two or three come together in my name, there am I with them'. In a different situation Jesus called a child to him and had him stand among them.

Then he said that 'whoever welcomes a little child like this in my name, welcomes me' (Matthew 18:5). We are to recognise Christ in the children who are present, in the singing company, even in the babies who sometimes distract us.

But when we turn to Matthew 25:31-44 we are asked to do more than see Christ in our relationships with other Christians. We are to see Christ in the person who comes knocking at the hall door and interrupts with his need. It might be someone wanting clothes or food or shelter. It might be someone released from prison. Jesus says: 'I tell you the truth, whatever you did for one of the least of these brothers of mine, you did for me' (v 40). Christ comes to our meeting and is present among us in different ways. Worship and service come together.

As we recognise Christ in one another, as we are aware of his presence in the meeting, as we look to him for example, it should naturally follow that we become more like him and that when people look for Christ in us they will find him. The meeting will have been worthwhile, the vital encounter have made its impact.

Questions:

1. How can we ensure that we experience a vital personal encounter with Christ in our meetings?

2. In what ways do we approach and recognise Christ in our worship?

3. How does worship in our meetings relate to the way in which we live our everyday lives?

4. How relevant is our worship to newcomers? How much would they understand and what should we do to assist them?

Scripture to consider:

Deuteronomy 5:7, Isaiah 1:11-18, Psalm 95:6 and 96:9, John 4:21-24.

14

Call to
God's Word

We call Salvationists worldwide to a renewed and relevant proclamation of and close attention to the word of God, and to a quick and steady obedience to the radical demands of the word upon Salvationists personally, and upon our Movement corporately.

We affirm that when the gospel is preached God speaks. The Bible is the written word of God. Preaching is that same word opened, read, proclaimed and explained. When in our human weakness and foolishness we faithfully proclaim and explain the word, the world may hear and see a new thing; God speaks and God acts. To respond in obedient faith results in a decisive encounter with God. We affirm that God speaks profound truth in simple words, common language and potent metaphor, and we confess that at times our words, too often shallow, obscure, archaic or irrelevant, have veiled, not revealed, our God.

IT isn't by accident that The Salvation Army's first doctrine centres on the word of God: 'We believe that the Scriptures of the Old and New Testaments were given by inspiration of God, and that they only constitute the Divine rule of Christian faith and practice.'

Without the Scriptures we would be lost. The Scriptures give direction, correction, challenge, command, hope, explanation and foundation for living. Scripture is God's truth for his world. Its words bring life. Its pages confirm the possibility of forgiveness, salvation, renewal and empowering for living as God intends his people to live. Its messages are never exhausted. There is always more to find, more to take in, more to live by. To explore Scripture is to embark on an adventure that goes on and on, challenging both mind and heart, and promising God's presence throughout the journey.

In *Marching On!* Ted Palmer writes: 'The Salvation Army has served God with authority and success over the years because it is motivated by the word of God, structured according to the principles of those same Scriptures and ready to evaluate what it is doing or not doing according to God's commandments in the Bible.' These are encouraging words, but the reverse will also be true. Neglect of the word of God cannot help but diminish authority and success. If the Bible is not at the heart of all that the Army is and does, the Army will undoubtedly fail in its mission. No other words, however appealing or cleverly expressed, will be of use, unless they are in harmony with the word of God.

This is why the Commission urges a renewed and relevant proclamation of the word of God. This is why it asks for our close attention to the word of God. It calls for a quick and steady obedience to its demands – both personal and corporate. The Commission has a conviction that every corps should take time to answer the following question thoroughly: 'How can we as a corps ensure that we keep the word of God at the centre of our life together?' To establish this as a priority, to explore together how this can be achieved, is to ensure that the heart of the corps is beating soundly.

Voicing the Commission's feelings, Dr Roger Green says: 'It is beyond question that the great revivals of the Church, beginning with the Church in Jerusalem, came by the power of the Holy Spirit through the proclamation of the gospel, and such continues to be the case now. We are not without biblical and historical evidence of the importance of preaching. Our reason and our experience also confirm this view. Our corps were called preaching stations in The Christian Mission, giving evidence of the importance of preaching in our history.'

William Sangster wrote: 'Preaching . . . is the highest, holiest activity to which a man can give himself: a task which angels might envy and for which archangels might forsake the courts of Heaven.' In contrast, Anthony Trollope decided that the preaching clergyman could well be the bore of his age.

Bearing all this in mind, Captain John Read suggests that five issues constantly require discussion:

- The theology – or lack of it – undergirding the proclamation.
- Study time – or lack of it.
- The grounding of the word in an effective pastoral ministry.
- The need for evaluation and assessment.
- The necessity for topics that are earthed.

Some preaching can hardly be called preaching. What is presented from a platform or a pulpit is not always worthy of the name. Poor preparation or ill-judged irrelevancies can cheapen what should be precious.

As to those who listen, those who hear the word spoken, Lieut-Colonel Linda Bond suggests that their 'attitude of heart must be that of thanksgiving, faith, obedience, dependence. We don't sit above the word in judgement, nor do we worship it as a god, practising bibliolatory, but we come as learners, keen to listen, committed to obey. And this is with the understanding that the Spirit, who inspired the word, illumines our hearts and minds.'

Preaching and study of God's word are seen as vital to the life of the Church. Both are complemented today by a plethora of resources – videos, audio cassettes, books, seminars and courses. At whatever stage we are in our spiritual development, materials are available to assist us. There need be no excuse for neglecting the word of God.

The psalmist was convinced of its value: 'Your word is a lamp to my feet and a light for my path' (Psalm 119:105). In the same psalm we read: 'Your word, O Lord, is eternal; it stands firm in the heavens' (v 89). Writing to Timothy in the early days of the Church, the apostle Paul declared that the holy Scriptures 'are able to make you wise for salvation through faith in Christ Jesus' (2 Timothy 3:15).

With numerous translations of the Bible available to help our understanding, we may reflect on what William Booth said shortly after the *Revised Version* had been introduced in 1881:

'I want to see a new translation of the Bible into the hearts and conduct of living men and women. I want an improved translation – or transference it might be called – of the commandments and promises and teaching and influence of this Book to the minds and feelings and words and activities of the men and women who hold it to be an inspired book, and the only authorised rule of life.'

If the word of God is to rule our lives we must study it, heed it – and live by it!

Through the centuries of the Old Testament, God was seen speaking to his people through the Law and the prophets. When his word was heeded his people flourished. When they neglected his word they reaped the consequences of their neglect.

Words were, in fact, not enough. God sent his Son – the Word of God – to speak his words personally. We have some of those life-giving words recorded for our guidance and inspiration in the New Testament. We see that God's Son, Jesus Christ, not only meant what he said, but also lived out those words – even to the cost of his own life.

Life-giving though his words were and are, Jesus knew that words alone were not enough to meet the need of mankind. Ultimately he spoke through his actions. He spoke supremely through his sacrificial death on the cross. The word was love – unconditional, total, wholehearted, self-giving love. The Word spoke with his life.

As always, faithful preachers speak words from the word of God on behalf of *the* Word of God, who, through the Holy Spirit, indwells them. The preacher who stands on the platform must be the same person who shakes hands at the door, or is seen in the street the next day. All preachers must demonstrate the Word of God within them, motivating, refining. The Word of God must be witnessed in the lives of those who declare him – and receive him.

Questions:

1. How can we as a corps ensure that we keep the word of God at the centre of our life together?

2. How well-equipped are we to answer questions from enquirers about our faith?

3. In what ways does God act through his inspired word today?

4. What practical steps can we take to ensure that we interpret Scripture correctly and relate it to our own discipleship?

Scripture to consider:

Psalm 119:105-112, John 1:1-10, 2 Timothy 4:1-5,
1 Peter 3:15.

Call to
the Mercy Seat

We call Salvationists worldwide to recognise the wide understanding of the mercy seat that God has given to the Army; to rejoice that Christ uses this means of grace to confirm his presence; and to ensure that its spiritual benefits are fully explored in every corps and Army centre.

We affirm that the mercy seat in our meetings symbolises God's unremitting call to his people to meet with him. It is not only a place for repentance and forgiveness, but also a place for communion and commitment. Here we may experience a deep awareness of God's abundant grace and claim his boundless salvation. The mercy seat may be used by anyone, at any time, and particularly in Army meetings when, in response to the proclaimed word, all are invited to share loving and humble communion with the Lord.

A FORMER Salvation Army officer, now a minister in another denomination, was asked what he missed most about The Salvation Army. His reply was immediate and heartfelt. 'What I miss most is the privilege of inviting people to the mercy seat at the end of the sermon.' He had been used to concluding his preaching with a direct invitation for the congregation to make a public response. The call to the mercy seat was not part of his new church's tradition.

Put in its biblical perspective, the mercy seat was a solid gold cover for the Ark of the Covenant, which moved with the Israelites each time they changed location on their journeys (Exodus 25). It symbolised the presence of God among them (v 8). The mercy seat was on the top of the ark and in the ark were placed the Ten Commandments. 'There I will meet with you, and I will speak with you from above the mercy seat' (v 22, *RAV*), said the Lord. The mercy seat was seen as a meeting place between God and his people. The Salvation Army mercy seat is also a place where people meet God and talk with him.

Placed in its historical context within the Church, the origins of the modern mercy seat can be found in the 'mourner's bench' which was used in early 19th century revival meetings in the USA. Its use in one of William P. Chandler's meetings was explained in the following way:

'It was a great advantage because, with the seekers scattered all through the congregation, it was difficult to give them suitable attention. By bringing them together they were accessible to those who desired to instruct and encourage them.'

By the time Charles Finney campaigned in England in 1849, the mourner's bench was being referred to as the 'anxious seat'. The first issue of *The War Cry* (1879) used the term penitent-form:

'The General was again in charge at the Livingstone Hall and they had a very excellent meeting. After both services the usual prayer meeting was held. About 20 persons came forward to the penitent-form.'

There is little doubt that the penitent-form was intended for use by penitents seeking salvation. It was not merely 'a place of prayer'. Writing to his son Bramwell in 1876, William Booth said: 'In dealing with the anxious let no one be urged to go forward to the penitent-form who is not deeply convinced of sin and thoroughly earnest for salvation. The more thoroughly persons are awakened and broken down before God, the more readily they will exercise faith in Christ and enter into rest, and the more stable they will become afterwards.'

The terms 'mercy seat' and 'penitent-form' seem to have been interchangeable since the Army's earliest days. The Founder was among those who used both terms irrespective of reasons for its use. In *The Founder Speaks*, we find him saying: 'In a remarkable meeting I held in one of the large cities of Japan, during my visit to that country, a dear woman came to the mercy seat. She found forgiveness for herself, and went straight from the registration room to the place where she had been sitting, brought her two children to the penitent-form and, kneeling between them, pointed them to the Saviour whom she had just found.'

Through the years the mercy seat has found a wider use. It is still a place where the sinner finds pardon. It is also used for many spiritually-enriching purposes. *Orders and Regulations for Officers* states:

'The penitent-form or mercy seat (and, where used in holiness meetings, the holiness table) occupies an important place in Salvation Army activities. No virtue attaches to either of these as such, but they provide a place for confession, or for repentance, or for consecration, as well as for spiritual guidance to be given to any seeker.

'All who come to the penitent-form or mercy seat are described as seekers. Those who come forward for salvation are known as penitents, and backsliders seeking restoration can be described in the same way. A penitent who rises from his knees believing that his sins are forgiven is known as a convert. Anyone who leaves the mercy seat without such assurance can still be described as a seeker.

'A holiness seeker is one who desires to enter into the experience of sanctification.'

We see then that the mercy seat is a place for confession, repentance, consecration and spiritual guidance. When the International Spiritual Life Commission calls for Salvationists to 'recognise the wide understanding of the mercy seat that God has given to the Army', it is emphasising that 'it is not only a place for repentance and forgiveness, but also a place for communion and commitment'. It continues: 'Here we may experience a deep awareness of God's abundant grace and claim his boundless salvation. The mercy seat may be used by anyone, at any time, and particularly in Army meetings when, in response to the proclaimed word, all are invited to share loving and humble communion with the Lord.'

In a sense, there can be as many reasons for using the mercy seat as there are human needs. This is why the Commission speaks of ensuring that 'its spiritual benefits are fully explored in every corps and Army centre'.

Colonel Phil Needham in *Community in Mission* says:

'I think the mercy seat should be utilised for any purpose involving prayer. I think it is quite useful for Salvationists to be invited to come together for prayer at the mercy seat for a number of purposes. Unfortunately, in too many corps coming to the mercy seat means that there is something wrong or there has been a distressing defeat in the person's life. Having Salvationists together in positive prayer around the mercy seat can help remove some of the unfortunate barriers.'

Commissioner Wesley Harris (R) writing in *Battlelines* says:

'We may kneel to give thanks, to intercede for others, to dedicate ourselves, and to share spiritual communion with Christ, and whatever our need we can be assured that God can meet it.' He also describes the mercy seat as a place of 'grace, not disgrace'.

The act of kneeling shows humility, dying to self and submission to God. The act of standing after an encounter with God can also symbolise being raised to new life.

Phil Needham continues:

'The mercy seat itself is symbolic of any place where a seeker after God comes in prayer. The true mercy seat is of the heart, and the outward act of kneeling at a prayer bench, or any other place, is nothing if not the outward sign of a kneeling soul.'

He goes on to suggest that 'almost any place can become a mercy seat because where God chooses to speak to us and we are open to respond to him is in fact a mercy seat setting. The actual mercy seat in a corps hall is therefore only symbolic in the sense that it represents all such places.'

This is something with which the Army's early-day holiness teacher Commissioner Samuel Logan Brengle would heartily agree:

'I have carried a penitent-form around in my heart for half a century or more. And if there is ever any need, I constantly fly there,' he said.

It is also important to emphasise what the mercy seat is not. It is not the only place where people may meet with God. It is not the only place where sinners find salvation or forgiveness. It does not possess any special spiritual power of its own, nor is it a sacred object in the sense that it adds eternal significance to what takes place there. Its use is not an essential step which must be taken on the way to becoming a soldier in The Salvation Army.

This is made clear in *Orders and Regulations for Corps Officers,* which states:

'The sources from which new soldiers may be drawn are:

a) Seekers at the Army's penitent-form.

b) Those converted and prepared for soldiership through the instrumentality of the young people's work.

c) Persons already converted, who receive spiritual blessing, such as entire sanctification, and who feel called by God to serve in the ranks of the Army.'

The Army's use of the mercy seat arose naturally, as part of its integral mission and worship. Although Salvationists may sometimes be tempted or even requested to suggest which sacraments the use of the mercy seat covers, they ought not to look for identical church equivalents. The Founder did not look to base the practice of the Army on the structural beliefs of other churches, even though the Army's close identification with Methodism is acknowledged.

Adult baptism (an outward sign of allegiance to Christ) and Holy Communion (receiving grace) reflect something of what may happen during mercy seat encounters, but the mercy seat was not, and is not, a substitute for any other form of worship.

For Salvationists the mercy seat symbolises God's unremitting call to his people to meet with him. It is a reminder. It is an opportunity. It is a privilege.

General Albert Orsborn had no doubts:

'There are those who tell us that the hope of The Salvation Army for the future is in its young people. I do not agree with that. The hope of the Army is in the penitent-form. As soon as that goes out of use we go out. The sign of the finger of God on the mercy seat is the crowning glory of God's favour on The Salvation Army. The primary aim of Salvationists . . . must be the bringing of sinners to the mercy seat. Every meeting held, every programme presented, every contact made must be a means to this end – the salvation of souls.'

General Orsborn's passion and conviction that the mercy seat should play its part in helping sinners find salvation is still at the heart of the Movement. Week by week thousands of people throughout the world respond to the voice of God and kneel at an Army mercy seat. Some are turning to God for the first time, others are returning. Some come to seek guidance, others to confirm their dedication for a specific decision. There are prayers made for friends, spiritual hopes shared with the Lord and a sense of communion in just being with the God whose blessing is sought.

Through it Christ confirms his presence in our lives and we show our desire to find in him the spiritual resources he waits to supply

Questions:

1. What does the mercy seat mean to us today?

2. List reasons for which the mercy seat can be used.

3. If, as a corps, we explore its spiritual benefits, how would this affect our worship and response to God?

4. How well do casual attenders understand the place of the mercy seat in our life together? What should be done to help them in this regard?

Scripture to consider:

Exodus 25:20-22, 1 Corinthians 6:19, 20,
Ephesians 2:19-22, Hebrews 10:19-25.

Call to
Celebrate Christ's Presence

We call Salvationists worldwide to rejoice in our freedom to celebrate Christ's real presence at all our meals and in all our meetings, and to seize the opportunity to explore in our life together the significance of the simple meals shared by Jesus and his friends and by the first Christians.

We affirm that the Lord Jesus Christ is the one true sacrament of God. His incarnation and continuing gracious presence with his people by means of the indwelling Holy Spirit is the mystery at the heart of our faith. We hear our Lord's command to remember his broken body and his outpoured blood as in our families and in our faith communities we eat and drink together. We affirm that our meals and love feasts are an anticipation of the feasts of eternity, and a participation in that fellowship which is the body of Christ on earth.

IN Chapter 1 of *The Salvation Army Ceremonies Book* officers are reminded of some Salvation Army principles:

'The setting of fixed forms of words or acts in connection with the ceremonies is not part of the Salvationist's tradition. Further, there are many local customs in certain countries which necessitate some variation in the wording set out in this manual. Therefore, as long as Army principles and any legal requirements . . . are observed the officiating officer need not feel compelled to follow the suggested wording in such a way as would prevent his looking to God and relying upon him for ultimate guidance.'

Not surprisingly, there follows a reminder that this 'does not mean that the text can be so changed that essential Salvationist emphases are lost'.

When the Commission began its concluding discussions on the Sacraments it had a united premise from which to start. Everyone was agreed that God's grace is freely and readily accessible to all people at all times and in all places. There was also agreement that no particular outward observance is necessary to inward grace. These beliefs are at the heart of Salvation Army worship and practice. They are uncomplicated. They remind us of our individual contact (relationship) with God.

When the sacrament of Holy Communion is perceived by some Christians to have a higher (some churches say essential) status for the receiving of inward grace, complications are introduced. And when some suggest that Salvationists are spiritually 'incomplete' without this observance, care needs to be taken to see exactly what are the issues involved.

Underlying the Call to celebrate Christ's real presence at all our meals and in all our meetings is the belief that his presence can be enjoyed anywhere, at any time, by anyone.

When someone comes into relationship with Jesus Christ and is born of the Spirit, that person's life is changed. That person is indwelt by God himself. The relationship is established. The apostle Paul frequently spoke of this relationship: 'So then, just as you received Christ Jesus as Lord, continue to live in him, rooted and built up in him, strengthened in the faith' (Colossians 2:6,7). Later in the same letter he urges: 'Let the peace of Christ rule in your hearts, since as members of one body you were called to peace. And be thankful. Let the word of Christ dwell in you richly' (3:15,16). In his letter to the Galatians, Paul speaks of the most intimate of relationships: 'I have been crucified with Christ and I no longer live, but Christ lives in me. The life I live in the body, I live by faith in the Son of God, who loved me and gave himself for me' (2:20).

There have been times and there are occasions when some Christians suggest that Christ is 'received' during specific ceremonies or within certain forms of worship, or because certain elements are used. But the word 'received' is misleading. If Christ already indwells, we need no ceremony to 'receive' him. There are forms of worship which help us appreciate more deeply the presence of God in our lives, or which assist us in being more aware of his working within us, but the presence of the indwelling Christ is already established and it is this which matters above all else. Whatever forms of worship are employed to assist us, they should never be seen as essential in themselves.

The Commission asked if the Army was being 'disobedient' to the Lord's words as recorded in Luke 22:20 when at supper Jesus said: 'Do this in remembrance of me.' In considering this, the obvious first question to ask is, 'Do what?'

It is worth noting that Jesus was among friends sharing a Jewish custom when he was recorded as saying, 'Do this.' He was in a home, not a church. He was at a meal table, not a communion rail. He did not say that communion could only be administered by ordained priests. When we look at the question 'Do what?' we should not assume that the pattern adopted by any particular church is the answer. Different churches have responded differently. Which approach is right? When the Church has been divided through the centuries, it has generally been because too much emphasis has been put on the form of observance rather than on the observance itself.

The Commission decided unanimously that the Army was not being disobedient to the Lord's words.

There was, however, a strong feeling that although remembrance of the Lord's death has always been at the heart of Salvation Army worship and motivation for service, the Army has not always used its freedom to demonstrate this in its meetings and in its family groupings.

New impetus is needed to ensure that opportunities to recognise Christ's presence, and to remember his atonement, are used as often as possible to deep and spiritually-enriching effect. Among ways in which this can be achieved is the encouraging of fellowship meals.

Fellowship meals do not depend upon set forms of words, and they provide opportunity for creative worship and participation. They can be adapted to particular cultures. The hallowing of meals at home was felt to have been neglected, yet they could be of great spiritual value within families. It was recognised that such meals are more easily practised in some cultures than others. (Commission members had to keep in mind that the report was to embrace 104 different countries.)

Another important point is that the same terms mean different things in different cultures and countries. For instance, 'the Lord's Supper' does not have the same meaning in Brazil as in England or in France. The same applies to 'Holy Communion', 'Agape' and 'Love Feast' in other places.

The Commission also felt it important to emphasise that when Salvationists attend other Christian gatherings in which a form of Holy Communion is included, they should feel free to partake if the host church allows. Such sharing in fellowship plays a positive part in the total life of the Church. The Commission discovered that, over the years, some territories had actively discouraged any such participation. Contrast this with some areas of South America where the cultures assume that water baptism and participation in the Lord's Supper are 'essential', and it will be appreciated that Commission members felt deeply the contrasting needs of different areas of the Army world.

William Booth practised the sacrament of Holy Communion after he was ordained in the Methodist ministry, and throughout his leadership of the Army he was always careful not to dismiss the spiritual benefits felt by those who took communion. Speaking to a congregation of Salvation Army officers in council in Melbourne soon after the Army had begun to establish itself in Australia, he confirmed: 'I never allow myself to be led into conversation at the dinner table or to say one word to make anybody else think less of the Sacraments than they do.' But of those who might suggest that sacraments were essential to salvation – and there were more than a few – he said: '. . . but do not let them interfere with your liberty.'

It is this liberty – this freedom – to which the Commission now draws attention. There are many ways in which the Lord's death and presence among his people can be remembered.

The preaching of the cross was at the centre of the apostle Paul's ministry (1 Corinthians 1:23). It must always be at the heart of the Army's life and worship. Although no specific elements are necessary to such emphasis, a variety of approaches can be used by God to assist our understanding.

So the Commission urges Salvationists 'to seize the opportunity to explore in our life together the significance of the simple meal shared by Jesus and his friends and the first Christians'. Key words such as 'seize', 'opportunity' and 'explore' featured in the early-day Army when faith was a new adventure for the Movement, and God was opening doors with a frequency which captured the world's attention.

During the visit of Bishop (Dr) John Austin Baker, a former Chairman of the Church of England's Doctrine Commission, he reminded Commission members that the Army possessed a glorious freedom to explore. He asked them to appreciate what a blessing this was. The Army had not tied itself down to specific forms of worship and words, nor had it given ceremonies an importance which they did not merit. He advised against introducing any sacrament in order to be like other churches.

The more the Commission looked at this, the more it felt that the privileges of exploration and freedom were not always being used to best effect in the Army of today. Many Salvationists had 'settled down', become predictable, even reluctant sometimes to see what new things God could do for them within the freedom which he had given.

Some Salvationists had mistakenly supposed that the Army was *anti*-sacramental, that it was opposed either to other Christians finding spiritual benefit in such forms of worship or to Salvationists accepting the invitation to partake at inter-denominational events. This view needed to be rectified.

It is all-too-possible to carelessly take the presence of Christ for granted when a company of believers meets. The wonder of his atoning sacrifice can, sadly, become a familiar piece of information rather than something felt deeply in the heart. The Call by the Commission to look again at ways in which Christ's real presence is celebrated at our meals and in our meetings urges Salvationists to ensure that the most selfless event of all time – Christ's sacrificial death – is kept firmly at the heart of all that the Army is and its people are. In order to assist with this, the Commission has not only suggested a wider use of fellowship meals but also listed a number of ways in which they can be shared. The Commission has also been careful to leave room for freedom of thought and expression, and the list on page 33 reflects this.

In his address in Melbourne, William Booth took to task those who were criticising the Army for not observing the Sacraments. But as he did so he revealed something of the experience of the Army's early-day soldiers. He demonstrated how their lives spoke of their relationship with the Lord:

'Take a Salvation Army corps. Look at it. You begin at the 7 o'clock knee-drill and take hold of Jesus. You say, "Oh, Jesus, your blood is our cleansing; your Holy Ghost is going to help us today." Then you go into the open-air at 10 o'clock – indoors again for the holiness gathering. Then you go out again in the afternoon to fight . . . You struggle through your night meeting. Supposing I were to call you together after all this day's pleading and wrestling and feeling about the cleansing blood, and say to you, "Come and take this to help you remember Jesus Christ." The soldiers would say: "It is ridiculous. . . He is in our hearts."'

There was little doubt that the Salvationists described by William Booth were making their lives their sacrament – whether they were aware of this or not.

General Albert Orsborn's expressive song 'My Life Must Be Christ's Broken Bread' may be easier to sing than to put into practice. At its heart are the prayer and intention which Salvationists confirm and live out when being true to their calling:

> *My life must be Christ's broken bread,*
> *My love his outpoured wine,*
> *A cup o'er filled, a table spread*
> *Beneath his name and sign,*
> *That other souls, refreshed and fed,*
> *May share his life through mine.*
>
> *My all is in the Master's hands*
> *For him to bless and break;*
> *Beyond the brook his winepress stands*
> *And thence my way I take,*
> *Resolved the whole of love's demands*
> *To give, for his dear sake.*
>
> *Lord, let me share that grace of thine*
> *Wherewith thou didst sustain*
> *The burden of the fruitful vine,*
> *The gift of buried grain.*
> *Who dies with thee, O Word divine,*
> *Shall rise and live again.*

Christ's body was broken for us. Whatever form of worship we use to remember his supreme act of love and salvation, we are called to use our lives in his service and for his sake. To give, to share, to die – and live again.

Perhaps we should give the Founder the last word:

'Let us do all that we do in remembrance of his dying love. Every act of our life ought to be religious. Every day ought to be a Sabbath in the sense of its being sacred and devoted to the glory of God, and every meal we take ought to be a sacrament.

'Look not only on the form and ceremonies; read your New Testament, not only with an eye on what I have told you, but settle it in your souls – that the Kingdom of God does not come by might nor by power; for the Kingdom of God is not meat and drink, it is not sacraments, nor ceremonials, not forms, not church attendance, not processions, not uniforms. The Kingdom of God is within you. It cometh not with observation. It is not what you can see or hear – the *essence* of it is not. Outside things may help you. They do help me very much. The countenances of my comrades help me, so do their songs, their faith, their devotion. The crash of a great big meeting, when hearts are yielded and souls are shouting the praises of God, helps me. But the power is not in these things. The Kingdom of God is righteousness, peace and joy in the Holy Ghost.'

Questions:

1. What ensures our recognition of Christ's real presence in our meetings and at our meals?

2. How does our worship reflect the truth that God's grace is freely and readily available to all people, at all times and in all places?

3. How well do we understand and live out the truth of 'Christ in me'?

4. Which of the suggestions for fellowship meals would most enrich our corporate life in Christ?

Scripture to consider:

Matthew 26:26-30, Luke 24:30-32, Colossians 2:6-10 and 3:15-17, Titus 3:4-7.

Fellowship Meals

Recognising that every meal may be hallowed, whether in the home or with a congregation, there are strategic occasions when the planning of a fellowship meal may especially enrich corporate spiritual life. Such occasions could include the following:

● In preparation for and during the Easter period.

● At the beginning of a mission or spiritual campaign.

● At a corps celebration such as an anniversary, a New Year's Eve watchnight service, or the opening of a new building.

● At a soldiers' meeting.

● For the pastoral care council (census board) or corps council, particularly when important decisions need to be made.

● For the launching of an annual appeal when the significance of work/service being undertaken in Christ's name could be emphasised.

● Harvest thanksgiving.

● Between meetings when a meal is required and members of the congregation are unable to travel home to eat because of distance.

● When there has been a breakdown in relationships and healing is sought by reflecting on Christ's great act of reconciliation through the cross.

● Whenever it is thought that such a gathering would strengthen the spiritual life and wider fellowship of the corps or centre.

● Small group meetings, especially house groups, midweek meetings or (for example) at the conclusion of a recruits' preparation for soldiership course.

● Corps camps, fellowship weekends or retreats.

Two features of the common fellowship meal in the early New Testament Church were the scope for spontaneity and the element of charity, with the poor being included. These elements are also worth noting.

Call to Soldiership

We call Salvationists worldwide to recognise that the swearing-in of soldiers is a public witness to Christ's command to make disciples and that soldiership demands ongoing radical obedience.

We affirm that Jesus Christ still calls men and women to take up their cross and follow him. This wholehearted and absolute acceptance of Christ as Lord is a costly discipleship. We hear our Lord's command to make disciples, baptising them in the name of the Father, the Son and the Holy Spirit. We believe that soldiership is discipleship and that the public swearing-in of a soldier of The Salvation Army beneath the Army's Trinitarian flag fulfils this command. It is a public response and witness to the life-changing encounter with Christ which has already taken place, as is the believers' water baptism practised by some other Christians.

FIRST let us remind ourselves again of something that relates to any public profession of faith, anything which acknowledges our becoming members of Christ's Church on earth. The public witness is to a life-changing encounter with Christ *which has already taken place*. The swearing-in ceremony of a Salvation Army soldier or the water baptism of a Baptist, or an equivalent ceremony in the Methodist Church or that of any other denomination, is a response to something which has already happened. The ceremony itself is not the conversion experience. Neither is it the defining factor in what is taking place. The ceremony has been planned and undertaken because of the experience into which the person concerned has already entered.

Whether or not new converts in the Early Church were usually baptised (with water) immediately they were saved, we cannot say for certain. We know that it happened on occasions. We also know that the apostle Paul did not see baptism as a priority in his own ministry (1 Corinthians 1:17). Nor did Jesus (John 4:2).

Through the years, however, initiation into the Church, being received as a member of the body of Christ, has become a planned occasion, and the forms in which this has taken place are many and varied. In most churches preparation is made to ensure the validity of the new Christian's experience and intention.

According to *The Salvation Army Ceremonies Book* the only people who may be received into soldiership are those who:

a) Have professed salvation through faith in Christ and now acknowledge him as Lord and Saviour.

b) Have studied the doctrines, principles and evangelistic witness of the Army as embodied in the articles of war (A Soldier's Covenant) and fully explained in *Chosen to be a Soldier* (*Orders and Regulations for Soldiers of The Salvation Army*) and *The Salvation Army Handbook of Doctrine*.

c) Have been accepted by the senior census board (pastoral care council) in accordance with *Orders and Regulations for Senior Census Boards*.

d) Have signed the articles of war (A Soldier's Covenant).

The way to soldiership is not a formality, nor should it be thought easy or be taken for granted.

The postmodern society of the West is not over-concerned about public witness or specific commitment. Those making the kind of undertakings required for soldiership are swimming against the tide.

So they are making a statement. A big one. And those Salvation Army soldiers who wear a uniform are, so to speak, in the firing line. You do not become a soldier to be anonymous. You do not become a disciple to have an easy life, and soldiership should only begin if the conversion experience is real and if the person concerned is empowered by the Holy Spirit's indwelling.

It is this indwelling which is all-important to soldiership. The swearing-in ceremony itself is a means to an end. It is a means whereby a new soldier professes new life in Christ and is welcomed formally into the life of the Church as expressed in The Salvation Army. It is a positive, God-blessed occasion. (The 'Statement on Baptism' in 'The Sacraments' section of this book explains this in concise detail.)

If the validity of the life-changing encounter with Christ has been established, a life with a difference awaits. Soldiership, says the Commission, demands ongoing radical obedience. It is inconceivable that a disciple would promise to follow Jesus and not expect to continue to obey the Master. The Army's ninth doctrine makes this clear:

'We believe that continuance in a state of salvation depends upon continued obedient faith in Christ.'

If Jesus, being in very nature God, made himself nothing and became *obedient unto death* – even death on a cross – his followers, if they hope to be worthy of their name, will expect also to be obedient and 'take up their cross and follow him'. The Commission draws attention to the wholehearted and absolute acceptance of Christ as Lord by every soldier and describes it as a militant, costly discipleship. If discipleship isn't costly, it isn't real discipleship.

So discipleship for a soldier includes the promise to be responsive to the Holy Spirit's promptings and obedient to his leading. It includes the intention to grow in grace through worship, prayer, service and the study of Scripture. There is the promise to make the values of the Kingdom of God and not the values of the world the standard for life. Christian integrity in every area, Christian ideals in all relationships, the sanctity of marriage and of family life are all at the heart of promises made. Stewardship of all a soldier has and is – body, mind and spirit – acknowledges an accountability to God.

It would be a strange kind of disciple who had no desire to share the good news of Jesus Christ with others. The endeavour to win people to him, and to care for the needy and disadvantaged, is acknowledged. For Salvation Army soldiers, abstinence from alcoholic drink, tobacco, the non-medical use of addictive drugs, gambling, pornography, the occult, and all else that could enslave the body or spirit, is accepted as spiritual discipline. Commitment to a corps and loyalty to the principles and practices of the Army, whether in times of popularity or persecution, are stated clearly too. Soldiership is not for the half-hearted.

Today a growing number of people find it helpful to join the ranks of adherents of The Salvation Army. Many carry through their discipleship without becoming soldiers. Their participation in the life of a corps, the life of the Army, the life of the Church, is welcomed, valued and acknowledged. Other adherents, not ready for discipleship, are nonetheless glad to be within the ministry and care of Salvation Army fellowship.

The Call for Salvationists to be 'God's People' recognises both the Army's uniqueness and its place in the life of the Church universal. The Founders of the Army were convinced that God had raised up the Movement to have its own defined role within the life of the Church. It has done so for approximately 135 years and continues to play an increasingly influential part in the world, being established in 104 countries.

Soldiership confirms commitment to the God who raised up the Movement and that commitment is best expressed through service to others. Without soldiers the Army would die. It depends on soldiers to fight the battle against evil. It needs soldiers who know God's hand of guidance is on them. It needs soldiers who dare to trust God with their lives. It needs soldiers who obey their Lord, and who know how to say 'Yes' to him. Whoever heard of an Army without soldiers?

Questions:

1. How important is our public witness to our life-changing encounter with Christ?

2. What happens to us at the moment of conversion?

3. How costly is our personal discipleship?

4. In what ways can we ensure that our obedience to the ongoing call of discipleship is maintained?

Scripture to consider:

Matthew 10:37-39, Mark 8: 34-37, John 3:3-8,
1 Corinthians 1:10-25 and 12:13, 2 Corinthians 6:1-10,
Ephesians 4:4-6.

Call to
the Inner Life

We call Salvationists worldwide to enter the new millennium with a renewal of faithful, disciplined and persistent prayer; to study God's word consistently and to seek God's will earnestly; to deny self and to live a lifestyle of simplicity in a spirit of trust and thankfulness.

We affirm that the consistent cultivation of the inner life is essential for our faith life and for our fighting fitness. The disciplines of the inner life include solitude, prayer and meditation, study, and self-denial. Practising solitude, spending time alone with God, we discover the importance of silence, learn to listen to God, and discover our true selves. Praying, we engage in a unique dialogue that encompasses adoration and confession, petition and intercession. As we meditate we attend to God's transforming word. As we study we train our minds towards Christlikeness, allowing the word of God to shape our thinking. Practising self-denial, we focus on God and grow in spiritual perception. We expose how our appetites can control us, and draw closer in experience, empathy and action to those who live with deprivation and scarcity.

THERE is no need to try and batter down the doors of Heaven with our prayers as if God's attention needed to be caught. That is what pagans do. Jesus warned his disciples not to be like them and told them that 'the Father knows what we need before we ask him' (Matthew 6:8). If we are aware of human need, or have concerns on our heart, we can be sure God is already ahead of us. God is also aware of our deepest inner needs, the needs of our spirit. He knows them better than we do and he is more ready to meet them than we are to bring them to him. The disciplines of the inner life, when applied, help us to discover what God wants to give us and make us. They can draw us closer to him, make us more aware of him and improve our perspective on life.

As the Call to all Salvationists reminds us: 'The vitality of our spiritual life as a Movement will be seen and tested in our turning to the world in evangelism and service, but the springs of our spiritual life are to be found in our turning to God in worship, in the disciplines of life in the Spirit, and in the study of God's word.'

In John 17, Jesus prays for himself, his disciples and for all believers. He reveals himself as the great intercessor. He prays to his Father for a unity, a oneness, a quality of relationship that wants to include everyone. Two thousand years ago Jesus is recorded as praying for us! As he prays for his disciples, he also prays for 'those who will believe in me through their message, that all of them may be one' (v 20, 21). He was interceding for us long before we existed. When we engage in prayer we draw closer to the One who is ever-ready to intercede for us (Hebrews 7:25).

And so, at the heart of any consideration of our spiritual life is prayer – faithful, disciplined and persistent prayer. William Cowper reminds us of its essential place in the Christian's life:

> *Restraining prayer, we cease to fight;*
> *Prayer makes the soldier's armour bright;*
> *And Satan trembles when he sees*
> *The weakest saint upon his knees.*

Understanding what prayer is, is another matter. Jean-Nicholas Grou in *How to Pray* compliments the disciples on their realisation that they needed to be taught how to pray:

'Ah! if we were only convinced of our ignorance and of our need of a teacher like Jesus Christ! If we would only approach him with confidence, asking him to teach us himself and desiring to be taught by his grace how to converse with God! How soon we should be skilled in it and how many of its secrets we should discover!'

When the disciples asked Jesus to teach them how to pray he taught them what we now call the Lord's Prayer. A brief analysis of the prayer shows that it gives God his rightful place, seeks at all times the good of his Kingdom and asks him for the spiritual qualities needed to live life as he intends. It is not a 'shopping list' of requests to assist us in having a trouble-free, favoured life. In the Lord's Prayer, God's will stands supreme and encourages the conclusion that 'Thy will be done' must always be at the heart of every prayer.

When Jesus invited his disciples to ask him for 'anything' in his name, the words 'in my name' were all-important. We are to ask for the things that will help his Kingdom grow.

Significantly, Mark chapter 10 records two incidents in which people came to Jesus with a request. James and John were straight to the point: 'We want you to do for us whatever we ask' (v 35). In effect they wanted power and recognition – not the kind of requests Jesus had in mind! By verse 51 of the same chapter, Blind Bartimeus is found making his request to be able to see. His request was granted. In both instances Jesus spoke the same words to those who came to him: 'What do you want me to do for you?' (v 36, 51). He asks the same today as we approach him in prayer and offers resources for our inner life, not power and recognition to enhance our reputation or standing.

In his paper on private devotions, Warren Johnson pointed out: 'One of the most important aspects of our devotional time is the desire to have it.' The psalmist expresses that longing: 'As the deer pants for streams of water, so my soul pants for you, O God' (Psalm 42:1). With this desire at the centre of our lives we come to know God and his plan for us. Prayer, we know, was at the heart of Jesus' life. We find in him our example. 'Very early in the morning, while it was still dark, Jesus got up, left the house and went off to a solitary place, where he prayed' (Mark 1:35).

Warren Johnson also asserted his conviction that the 'strength and spiritual vitality of The Salvation Army is in direct proportion to the commitment of its officers and soldiers to personal devotions and private prayer, and to applying God's words in our daily walk'.

Research among fellow-Salvationists and other Christians revealed that most people find prayer fulfilling when a helpful pattern is established. A logical order – adoration, confession, thanksgiving and supplication – is a valued procedure followed by many. Advice on prayer was shared – be determined to do it, make sure you prepare, develop a prayer journal, keep an alive intercessory prayer list, pray

41

with the aid of a devotional Bible reading, and use *The Song Book of The Salvation Army* to challenge, reassure or inspire you. While prayer can be informal, it should not be casual, undisciplined or slip-shod.

But it is possible to develop a prayer life which is removed from the way we live. Strange though it may seem, it is possible to develop a personally-enriching time with the Lord, yet fail to translate this into our daily living. The question, 'To what extent is my lifestyle an honest reflection of the prayers I speak?' (see end of chapter) is well worth answering. James Montgomery's song, 'Prayer is the soul's sincere desire, uttered or unexpressed', reminds us that our true prayer is what we feel deep within us. It is possible to say one thing with our lips, but lack the desire that matches our words. God knows when prayer is real and going to be proved sincere by the way we live.

A humbling, unifying and enriching aspect of prayer is that of remembering others. By taking time to bring people before the Lord we are showing a form of commitment to them. We are also giving God an opportunity to tell us how we might best help or support those for whom we pray. It is at this point that often we discover whether our prayers match our desires. Our true prayer is seen for what it is by our reaction or non-action to what the Lord is telling us.

The Call to 'study God's word consistently' can help ensure that our prayers are rooted in God's values and not our own. This is a useful safeguard. To dwell on one's own 'experience' of God without the underlying guidance of his word is to invite danger and distortion. The Commission's affirmation points out that 'as we meditate we attend to God's transforming word. As we study we train our minds towards Christ-likeness, allowing the word of God to shape our thinking.'

The Commission was asked to look at and identify various disciplines of the inner life. Solitude, fasting, spiritual retreats, the use of mentors or spiritual directors, study and meditation are all among disciplines which can enrich us and cultivate spiritual perception.

Lieut-Colonel Kehs-David Lofgren gave a word of caution to the Commission: 'Dangers to be guarded against include moralism – the attempt to make oneself worthy in the sight of God – and escapism – when you isolate yourself from people around you and move into a private world of contemplation. Another temptation is to be Pharisaical: the pretence of being more spiritual than you really are.'

Solitude involves spending time alone with God. We come to discover the importance of silence, learn to listen to God, and discover our true selves. Meditation gives opportunity for communion and conversation with God by some form of temporary withdrawal from everyday life, an attachment to God, a focus on Jesus, and a hearing of God's word.

Self-denial involves forgoing non-essentials in order to focus on God and the things of the Spirit. It can also expose how our appetites control us, and can bring us closer in experience, empathy and action to people who live with deprivation and scarcity all the time.

The spirit of this was reflected in early-day Salvationists who abstained from eating food themselves in order to feed the poor. This kind of action became formalised in the Self-Denial Appeal, but for some this eventually became a ritual and instead of abstaining they became more inclined simply to invite donations from non-Salvationists. Today, in a world where obtaining 'rights' is prominent, a life of self-denial can easily be avoided or overlooked.

Fasting may be thought a thing of the past in some Christian cultures, but the then Major N. J. Vijayalakshmi brought an Indian perspective to the Commission:

'To some Christians fasting appears to be extreme and fanatical, but the Bible is full of references to fasting. From the beginning, religion and fasting have been together. Religious fasting is not mere abstinence from food and drink, but is observed with frequent prayers and sacrifices of comforts. Luxuries, outings, sex, sleep and other factors which may enrich the body but cause distraction to time spent alone with God, are avoided in order to create a congenial atmosphere to lift up oneself into the divine presence and holiness of God.'

The Bible gives various indications of the value of fasting. When Moses fasted God gave him the Ten Commandments (Exodus 24:18). Elijah fasted when he was in despair and running away from Jezebel. God came to him in these moments (1 Kings 19:7, 8). David fasted for seven days in repentance; weeping and crying to God for the life of his dying son, born of his illegitimate intimacy with Bathsheba, wife of Uriah. Jesus himself fasted when facing temptations in the wilderness. These and other instances show the value of spending time with God.

Major Vijayalakshmi continued: 'There have been two opinions regarding the discipline of fasting – one that it is commanded, the other that it is recommended.' Thomas Cartwright, a distinguished Elizabethan Puritan, argued that 'fasting is an abstinence commanded of the Lord to make solemn profession of our repentance'. Opposing this view, John Brown wrote that Christ did not command these exercises, but 'proceeded on the principle that the children of the Kingdom would perform them'. Writing in *Studies in the Sermon on the Mount,* Dr Martyn Lloyd-Jones pointed out that Jesus spoke of *when* you fast, not *if* you fast (Matthew 6:16).

The danger of allowing fasting to be ruled by the self-centred principle – 'What do we get out of it from God?'– is also considered. Major Vijayalakshmi points out that 'there is so much emphasis on fasting for personal benefit – for the endowment of power, for spiritual gifts, for physical healing, for specific answers to prayer – that the most important aspect can be neglected. Fasting is unto-God. God is not merely concerned with what we do, but why we do it. Fasting is to honour and glorify God, and to accomplish his sovereign will.'

Mentoring or using a spiritual director to assist with spiritual development is proving to be of value to many Christians, especially leaders, in the pressurised modern world. The characteristics of a spiritual director have been defined as:

● A person possessed by the Spirit. The first essential characteristic of the spiritual guide is holiness of life, closeness to God.

● A person of experience, one who has struggled with the realities of prayer and life.

● A person of learning. St Teresa put learning as a high priority for spiritual guides. The guide must be one who is steeped in Scripture and 'in the wisdom of the Fathers'.

● A person of discernment.

● A person of perception, insight and vision.

● A person who knows how to give way to the Holy Spirit. An openness to the Holy Spirit is essential.

Spiritual direction is a means to an end, and the end is God, whose service is perfect freedom.

The value of spiritual retreats has been rediscovered in the Army in recent years. Whether for officers, corps groups or people in leadership positions, they have proved to be enriching and renewing, especially when business matters are excluded. A retreat not only brings people closer to God, it also provides opportunity for them to become closer to one another in fellowship and purpose. Through the years Salvationists have traditionally seemed too busy to consider sabbaticals, but in an increasingly pressurised and stressful world their value has become increasingly apparent.

Salvationists will always be busy. It is within the nature of Salvationists to work for God. We do not do so in order to earn our place in Heaven. That is not possible, nor is it necessary. But because we are active, we need also to guard time for being with God. If Jesus safeguarded his time with his Father, we know we should do the same. To attempt to do God's work without his guidance, without his strength, without his love, is to attempt the impossible.

Questions:

1. How can we each ensure that our prayer life is given priority each day?

2. In what ways can we ensure faithful, disciplined and persistent prayer is at the heart of our corps life?

3. To what extent is our lifestyle an honest reflection of the prayers we speak?

4. Are there new ways in which we can cultivate our inner life?

Scripture to consider:

Joel 2:12, Matthew 6:6 and 26:36-44, Luke 2:37,
Mark 1:35, 6:46 and 11:17, Ephesians 6:18,
Philippians 4:6, Colossians 4:2-4,
1 Thessalonians 5:17.

Call to
our Life Together

We call Salvationists worldwide to rejoice in their unique fellowship; to be open to support, guidance, nurture, affirmation and challenge from each other as members together of the body of Christ; and to participate actively and regularly in the life, membership and mission of a particular corps.

We affirm the unique fellowship of Salvationists worldwide. Our unity in the Holy Spirit is characterised by our shared vision, mission and joyful service. In our life together we share responsibility for one another's spiritual well-being. The vitality of our spiritual life is also enhanced by our accountability to one another, and when we practise the discipline of accountability our spiritual vision becomes objective, our decisions more balanced, and we gain the wisdom of the fellowship and the means to clarify and test our own thinking. Such spiritual direction may be provided effectively through a group or by an individual. Mutual accountability also provides the opportunity to confess failure or sin and receive the assurance of forgiveness and hope in Christ.

IT isn't an exaggeration, an overstatement, or a mistake to talk about The Salvation Army's 'unique fellowship'. However enriching, God-glorifying and spiritually effective other Christian fellowships are – and many are! – the fellowship which Salvationists enjoy has its own characteristics.

To begin with, the uniform identifies Salvationists. Although not worn by every Salvationist, its presence within the fellowship tends to have a bonding effect. From whatever country – say Uganda, Belgium, India or Canada – or from whatever position in life – say member of parliament, secretary, doctor or bus driver – and however wealthy or poor, healthy or sick, whether male or female, young or old, there is a shared identification which comes with the uniform. It is instantly recognisable among Salvationists and it would be rare indeed if there was not an immediate sense of belonging to one another when the uniform is seen. The uniform says 'we are all in this together'. It speaks of commitment to one another as well as to God. It plays a significant part in uniting the Army's soldiers, even when they may be unaware of it.

Consider also bands and songster brigades. They add to the sense of belonging and their significance is understood both worldwide and locally. Bandsmen and songsters share commitment to the fellowship, worship and evangelism. But there is also the danger that these 'uniting' fellowships can become exclusive and elitist. It is not unusual for people to feel excluded or diminished within a corps fellowship because they are not part of what is perceived to be an 'inner' group.

Then there is the structure. Territorial headquarters, divisional headquarters, corps or social centres – these are all significant in providing a means of communication within the Army. The periodicals produced by the Army link Salvationist with Salvationist and territory with territory. News spreads. A sense of shared concern, one for the other, is engendered. It is possible for news of an afternoon event in London to be travelling throughout the United States during the morning of the same day! There is genuine interest in each others' lives. All this can be extremely supportive. It can give a sense of security within fellowship and unity in Christ. At its best it is superb.

It can also have a 'downside'. There is a thin red line between genuine interest and gossip and intrigue. The tendency to want to know other people's business can lead to unhealthy concentration on what should be peripheral – the kind of matter that detracts from the God-inspired reasons for the Army's existence.

What else is unique? Divisional meetings, where Salvationists from various centres gather for holiness teaching or praise fellowships, do not have an equivalent in most other churches. Junior soldiership is in the same category. We give our children a part to play, if they choose to do so, in the great business of saving the world.

The office of General is particularly significant in providing a focus for reminding Salvationists everywhere that they belong together. A visit from the General is a special link the world over. Speaking in the early part of the 20th century General Evangeline Booth said: 'Each of us is an integral part of a vast circle that encompasses the globe. In this is our strength. Without it we are weak . . . this glorious unity must not perish.'

However, the real unity which counts, the one on which everything must be founded, is unity in the Holy Spirit. There is no other reason under Heaven why Salvationists should be united except in God and for his Kingdom's sake. When we examine the uniqueness of the fellowship we do so to ensure that it is being used and enjoyed to the best effect. The fellowship comes into its own when its members are 'open to support, guidance, nurture, affirmation and challenge from each other'. Recognising one another as members together of the body of Christ, Salvationists will see Christ in one another and respond accordingly.

Speaking to a Salvation Army officer on London Bridge, a flower-seller pointed to the International Headquarters building and made the accusation: 'You Salvationists are the richest people in the world!' He didn't realise the truth of his words. The officer to whom he was talking had little in his bank account at the time. The building to which he was referring had been paid for brick-by-brick by Salvationists from around the world – not from public funds. Nevertheless, the flower-seller's words rang true. Yes, Salvationists must be the richest people in the world. They know God, his pardon, his love, his support, his guidance, his strengthening, his peace and so much else. And with it all, a sense of belonging to the Kingdom of God, the richest fellowship possible. To feel support from other Christians is a tremendous privilege. It can come in times of distress, bereavement, injustice, misbehaviour, sorrow and loneliness. When accompanied by faithful prayer, it is twice-blessed.

The privilege of giving guidance to one another, of helping others on their way, or preventing them from making mistakes – all this is possible within the fellowship. Nurture, helping people grow in the faith, brings its own reward to the one who gives and the one who receives. It can be spiritually satisfying and life-enriching. The apostle Paul speaks of the value of such mutual support and of his joy being made complete by believers 'being like-minded, having the same love, being one in spirit and purpose' (Philippians 2:2). He continues: '. . . in humility consider others better than yourselves. Each of you should look not only to your own interests, but also to the interests of others' (v 3, 4).

The Commission also calls Salvationists to affirm one another. When someone is affirmed, reassured or told they are valued, it does them good! They feel better. They know they are of worth and have a part to play. Because they are appreciated, they are ready to give again. The father for whom nothing is ever good enough destroys confidence in his child and usually causes problems for later life. The Salvation Army leader or officer who fails to affirm people, or who belittles them instead, causes unnecessary problems and heartache. The Commission calls Salvationists everywhere to affirm one another in Christ and to enjoy the results.

There is also a call to challenge one another. Challenge can come in many ways. It comes from the pulpit every Sunday. The Bible is full of challenge, songs have their challenge and the Holy Spirit finds his own way of challenging his people. Challenge is the antidote to complacency, both personally and corporately. Christians who avoid it are avoiding living the Christian life. Christians also need to issue challenges and the challenges always carry more weight when the person issuing them pledges personal involvement too!

When Jesus was speaking to his disciples shortly before his crucifixion, he told them: 'By this all men will know that you are my disciples, if you love one another' (John 13:35). The Church has many ways of trying to show its unity. Some are successful, some not so successful. Hymns, prayers, ceremonies, rituals, missions, charity events, social service ministries and various campaigns all have their place, but the genuine way, the only way that counts, is if we love one another. Jesus said so. Without love, any support, guidance, nurture, affirmation or challenge will be defective. Given in love, genuine Christlike love, it will be used by Christ himself to effect his purposes.

When Jesus prayed for all believers, he lifted fellowship and 'oneness' to a new level. 'I pray also for those who will believe in me through their message, that all of them may be one, Father, just as you are in me and I am in you' (John 17:20, 21). Such closeness, such unity, such oneness is an ongoing challenge to Christians everywhere. It is an incredible privilege – but not for the exclusive few. It has been made possible for a purpose. Jesus continued: 'May they also be in us so that the world may believe that you have sent me . . . I have given them the glory that you gave me, that they may be one as we are one: I in them and you in me. May they be brought to complete unity to let the world know that you sent me and have loved them even as you have loved me' (v 22, 23).

The fellowship Jesus has in mind is all-embracing. His arms stretch round the world. So should ours, beginning at home.

Questions:

1. Are there ways in which Salvation Army fellowship seems unique or different from that found in other churches?

2. How can we ensure our unity in Christ?

3. How can we use our unity to best effect for support and nurture within the fellowship?

4. How committed are we to one another in Christlike love?

Scripture to consider:

John 13:34, 35 and 15:12, 1 Corinthians 12:14-20,
Ephesians 3:14-19, Philippians 2:1-5.

Call to
our Life in the World

We call Salvationists worldwide to commit themselves and their gifts to the salvation of the world, and to embrace servanthood, expressing it through the joy of self-giving and the discipline of Christlike living.

We affirm that commitment to Christ requires the offering of our lives in simplicity, submission and service. Practising simplicity we become people whose witness to the world is expressed by the values we live by, as well as by the message we proclaim. This leads to service which is a self-giving for the salvation and healing of a hurting world, as well as a prophetic witness in the face of social injustice.

WE have only to look at Jesus to see that simplicity and servanthood are at the heart of Christianity. Jesus not only warned against the dangers of putting too much emphasis on possessions, wealth or an indulgent lifestyle, he also showed by the way he lived that he meant what he said. He is our supreme example.

Paul reminds us of this with some powerful Scripture: 'Your attitude should be the same as that of Christ Jesus: Who, being in very nature God, did not consider equality with God something to be grasped, but made himself nothing, taking the very nature of a servant, being made in human likeness' (Philippians 2:5-7).

On more than one occasion Jesus felt the need to rebuke his disciples for wanting to be 'great' (Matthew 20:26). 'Whoever wants to become great among you must be your servant,' he told them. On the night of his crucifixion he left his disciples with a lesson in service. 'He got up from the meal, took off his outer clothing, and wrapped a towel around his waist. After that, he poured water into a basin and began to wash his disciples' feet, drying them with the towel that was wrapped around him' (John 13:4, 5). But even at this late hour in Jesus' ministry, Peter didn't understand what was going on. Jesus needed to explain. 'You call me "Teacher" and "Lord", and rightly so, for that is what I am. Now that I, your Lord and Teacher, have washed your feet, you also should wash one another's feet. I have set you an example' (v 13-15). He then reminded them that no servant was greater than his master! They were to take note of what he, their Lord and Master, was doing – and then live in the spirit of servanthood.

Two thousand years later the Church still needs to hear the Master's words. It is all too easy for those given authority to fall into the trap of thinking they are more important than others. If we can see problems emerging in the Early Church (James 2:3), it should come as no surprise to see ourselves making similar mistakes. Commission members were alive to this and have recommended that 'Salvation Army leadership at every level conform to the biblical model of servant leadership'. They recommended a re-evaluation of how effectively structures, ranks and systems encourage and support servant leadership, the spirit of community and the advancement of the Army's mission.

It should be noted that the recommendation addresses leadership 'at every level'. The spiritual obligations upon those in high office are also upon those who give leadership in corps and within other areas of Salvation Army ministry. If the question 'To what extent are self-giving and Christlike living evident in our fellowship?' (see end of chapter) is given careful and thorough attention within a corps fellowship, the Holy Spirit will have room to convict and challenge, and then show each fellowship how it can achieve the quality of servanthood that Christ desires.

The parable of the Good Samaritan (Luke 10:30-37) reminds us how easy it is for religious people to be so committed to their standards, practices and work schedules that they fail to make an impact in the real world – where their faith and service are most needed. Keeping up appearances, being seen to be doing the right thing at the right time and in the right way can stand in the way of doing what God actually requires.

The expert in the Law knew his Scripture well. He even told Jesus that to 'love the Lord your God with all your heart and with all your soul and with all your strength and with all your mind . . . and your neighbour as yourself' was the way to eternal life. But his reluctance to speak the word 'Samaritan' and give specific credit to a race Jews were known to despise, gave indication that although he knew in theory what was right, he wasn't prepared to put it into practice. Today's Christians have to guard against this vigorously.

In an age in which it has become popular and helpful to identify gifts for service, some have fallen into the trap of being selective. It makes sense to use the gifts God has given us, but to decline participation in some of the tasks by using 'It's not my gift' as an excuse means that servanthood can effectively be marginalised.

Paul speaks of beating his body and making it his slave (1 Corinthians 9:27), giving strong indication that discipleship isn't only about what comes naturally.

Today, where image seems to be all-important, we note that Jesus cared nothing for his image. He made himself 'nothing', Paul says. Jesus came into our world, into our mess, into our shoes and ultimately into our place. He embraced the cross. He made total identification with us. We who are made in God's image are invited to look at Jesus and discover that he became like us! In Song No 38 in *The Song Book of The Salvation Army* Albert Frederick Bayly makes this point:

> *You, Lord, have stamped your image on your creatures,*
> *And, though they mar that image, love them still;*
> *Lift up our eyes to Christ, that in his features*
> *We may discern the beauty of your will.*

But one thing leads to another. The affirmation which accompanies this Call says that 'practising simplicity we become people whose witness to the world is expressed by the values we live by, as well as by the message we proclaim'. It 'leads to service which is a self-giving for the salvation and healing of a hurting world, as well as a prophetic witness in the face of social injustice'. It isn't just about self-denial, it is about involvement – about doing something!

Warren Johnson contributes: 'Service is a practical ministry. It is not only a reaching into the body of believers with the heart of a servant, it is also a reaching out into a desperate and dying world with love in action.' He adds: 'A giant leap forward for the new believer is to comprehend the essence of God's call to men and women to serve and minister to those who cross our paths every day of the week. God wants to use us in the lives of other people.'

This was a theme which was taken further by Lieut-Colonel Margaret Hay when she presented a paper on social holiness. She reflected on a year 'living and working between a cosy, double-glazed quarters in London and IHQ, interspersed with journeys to places like Manila and Colombo'. She couldn't help but make contrasts. 'In Manila I looked through the car window into the faces of children inches from mine as we lurched through the choked streets only days after seeing choirboys in London, with flaxen hair crowning their neck-frills.'

She continued: 'In Colombo the Reverend Doctor Duleep Fernando, President of the Methodist Church, addressing the South Asia College for Officers, dared us to look at the face of the city and to see the face of suffering in a country where millions are dehumanised by poverty and war. In Colombo, he said, 60 per cent of the people live in abject poverty, half of those in cities live in slums, and research shows that among slum-dwellers, more than 50 per cent use public toilets, 16 per cent use neighbours' toilets, 15 per cent have their own, and nine per cent have none.

'Young slum-dwellers with ample time on their hands and little or no schooling have no role models except drug traffickers. The families come to the city with hope, but insecurity, fear and pessimism rise as their powerlessness, with no one to represent them, becomes evident. Such situations are also found in thousands of other world cities. People are harassed and helpless, caught between conflicting forces of violence, drought, pestilence and corruption.'

Dr Fernando gave a challenge to the delegates to look at the face of the Church where apathy, indifference and the values of the rich and middle-class seem to predominate. *'How often do Christians encounter the poor?'*

Colombo, with its overwhelming human need, may seem a long way away from daily living in the settings in which many Christians find themselves, but Christian theology respects all human life as sacred. However poor, retarded, sinful or disfigured, each person is stamped with God. If we identify God in others, we cannot help but act on their behalf whenever possible. The 'healing of a hurting world' and the need for 'prophetic witness in the face of social injustice', as advocated by the Commission, must be seen as more than wishful thinking.

Some of Major Campbell Roberts' thoughts were shared with the Commission:

'Cain's question, "Am I my brother's keeper?" in which he attempts to evade responsibility and deny the inter-connectedness of society, is responded to in unmistakable terms. God says that we *are* our brother's keeper – and he showed that overwhelmingly at Calvary.

'We who have received complete love from Christ are called to give transparent witness to justice, peace, equality and holiness through actions which redeem and re-order the world. We need to avoid mere words which spiritualise the gospel announcement of liberation, and cut it loose from rigorous social analysis. We need to follow our Lord in starting with the suffering of the poor and outcast, and expanding the scope of neighbourly love through the barriers of culture, religion, race, gender and nation. When proclamation and action match, the attractiveness and power of the gospel take hold.

'Since Christ brings the far-off near, and breaks down every dividing wall of hostility, the divided nature of our communities is not a Christian vision. A Christian vision is of people together, loving each other, sharing dreams and hopes, and counting on creative support. In Christ, no exclusion is tolerated as the Shepherd draws all into the circle. This is foundational teaching in a world where many are unanchored, uprooted and needing a place to land and stand.'

How, we may ask, does this vision square with the service we offer Christ?

The Commission affirms the joy of self-giving. God himself will affirm its value.

Questions:

1. How effectively are we using the gifts God has given us for the salvation of the world?

2. What are the servanthood values of the Kingdom by which we should live?

3. To what extent are self-giving and Christlike living evident in our fellowship?

4. How can God make us what we should be?

Scripture to consider:

John 13:3-17, 1 Corinthians 12:7-11 and 13:1-13,
2 Corinthians 8:9, Philippians 2:5-11,
Colossians 3:23, 24.

Call to
Cultivate Faith

We call Salvationists worldwide to explore new ways to recruit and train people who are both spiritually mature and educationally competent; to develop learning programmes and events that are biblically informed, culturally relevant, and educationally sound; and to create learning environments which encourage exploration, creativity and diversity.

We affirm that our mission demands the formation of a soldiery who are maturing, and are being equipped for faithful life and ministry in the world. In strategic and supportive partnership with the family, the Christian community has a duty to provide opportunities for growth into maturity by means of preaching and teaching, through worship and fellowship, and by healing and helping.

THERE are some exciting words in the Call to Cultivate Faith. Take note of them – explore, develop, create, encourage. There are some challenging phrases – new ways, training people, spiritually mature, educationally competent, biblically informed, culturally relevant, educationally sound. This Call cries out to be noticed, to be taken to heart, to be taken seriously, to be put into operation.

The Salvation Army cannot exist without people who are cultivating their faith. Without them there will be no real growth. Faith is not static. It must develop to stay alive. It must be exercised and it ceases to be faith unless it is applied. As years go by, it is possible for Christians to avoid situations which demand faith and settle for the comfort zone. The person who said that 'faith isn't faith until it is all we have' was making a vital point. It is only through trusting that we discover our faith is well-founded. There are times when the unfairness of life seems to attack us, to hold us in its grip, or to challenge the very foundations on which our lives have been built. It is then we discover the strength of our faith, or the lack of it. It is also the time when our faith can develop most rapidly and most surely.

Throughout The Salvation Army's history there have been some inspiring stories of personal courage and spiritual victory. Faith has held even in the most unlikely of circumstances. In fact, *because* adversity has necessitated dependence on God the result has been strengthened faith. The reverse has happened too. When people who have professed conversion and faith in the Lord Jesus have encountered times when his leadings have not been understood, when disappointment has emerged, or injustices have brought confusion, faith has gone 'out of the window'. The sad truth is that even some of those who have testified so convincingly of their faith in Christ, have fallen badly (even spectacularly) at unwelcome hurdles. Their knowledge of Scripture may have increased, their Christian service may have been given gladly, but their faith has not been cultivated. It has not been encouraged to grow.

There may have been a misunderstanding of God's promises – an assumption that following Jesus means freedom from trouble or distress, or that life would always seem fair. It may be that they have been misled by preachers or fellow-Christians who have given the impression that God is like a benevolent grandfather. They may not have realised that when Jesus told his disciples that 'in this world you will have trouble' he meant it and that when he asks people to 'take up their cross' and follow, he means that too. Spiritual growth frequently comes through suffering or coping with injustice, but those whose faith has not been thought through can find themselves spiritually lost.

When a Salvation Army uniform is donned for the first time, there can be a sense that the new soldier has 'arrived' spiritually. A subtle (even unnoticed) temptation to assume all will be well from now on may creep in, in spite of warnings in Scripture or from the platform to the contrary. If our quest for spiritual maturity is neglected, the day will eventually arrive when our spiritual poverty becomes evident.

Spiritual immaturity can be especially ugly. It is always disappointing and usually affects others. It brings inappropriate responses. It can be childish, rather than childlike. It manifests itself in outbursts, moaning or complaining. It looks for negatives rather than positives. It encourages people to think of themselves as victims rather than as people who can achieve or do something to remedy unhappy situations.

Spiritual immaturity demands that God puts right every little problem. It expects to be exempt from everyday difficulties or tragedies. It blames God or others – even 'the Army'! – when things go wrong. It is all too evident in our world and, sadly, sometimes within our fellowship. Shallow faith, which hasn't been thought through, will not be adequate when the day of testing comes. But it needn't be like this.

Those exciting words – such as 'explore', 'develop' and 'create' – indicate that anyone wanting to cultivate faith must be open to new ideas and concepts. Exploring, developing and creating are essential if we are to learn. The Christian who refuses to make faith a matter of mind as well as of heart will eventually become unable to give logical and convincing reasons for possessing faith. And the apostle Peter encourages us *always* to be ready to give a reason for the faith we hold dear (1 Peter 3:15). The apostle Paul promises that if we stay close to God, his peace will guard both our hearts *and our minds* in Christ Jesus (Philippians 4:7).

Intellectual laziness has nothing to commend it, yet the very busyness of Christian service can sometimes appear to encourage it. Almost imperceptibly, what began as Christian service can become activity for activity's sake. The heresy of trying to earn or work our way into Heaven takes over and is never satisfying – because it can't be done. Quiet times, study of the word of God, consistent openness to learning more about our great God and his ways, are essential to spiritual development.

For these reasons, the Commission makes its Call to Salvationists everywhere to identify people who are spiritually mature and educationally competent, and encourage them to put their gifts to good use. The Salvation Army needs teachers, it needs trainers, it needs people who will help others to learn. Never before have there been so many resources available for learning. People who know how to get the most out of them are required.

Creative programmes and approaches to education are available in packages to suit almost every kind of learning need. Learning doesn't have to be stuffy or boring. It should be inspiring, renewing and energising. It can result in new vision and new hope.

In this respect the Commission has welcomed the International Education Symposium, recently held in London. Drawing 40 Salvationist educationalists from around the world, the Symposium gave close attention to the question of how ongoing and far-reaching improvements can be made in faith education. The Commission's call for learning programmes and events that are biblically informed is in harmony with the Symposium's work.

Where faith is low or weak, biblical understanding is usually exposed as being weak too. The challenge to make learning programmes culturally relevant calls for both imagination and a real understanding of the world in which we live. The intellectually lazy or the self-centred will not accept the need for cultural relevance. But it is essential if the Army is to make any meaningful impact at local level. And just what *is* culturally relevant is best decided at corps level – but always with the guidance of the Holy Spirit.

Questions:

1. What does the spiritual maturity we seek involve?

2. How effective and at what depth is the teaching programme of our corps?

3. What training initiatives are being introduced and used in our corps?

4. What initiatives should be introduced to assist the cultural relevance of the programme and mission?

Scripture to consider:

Ephesians 4:11-16, Galatians 3:1-5,
1 Corinthians 3:1-9, James 1:5-8, 2 Timothy 2:15,
1 Thessalonians 2:13.

Call to
Holiness

We call Salvationists worldwide to restate and live out the doctrine of holiness in all its dimensions – personal, relational, social and political – in the context of our cultures and in the idioms of our day while allowing for, and indeed prizing, such diversity of experience and expression as is in accord with the Scriptures.

We affirm that God continues to desire and to command that his people be holy. For this Christ died, for this Christ rose again, for this the Spirit was given. We therefore determine to claim as God's gracious gift that holiness which is ours in Christ. We confess that at times we have failed to realise the practical consequences of the call to holiness within our relationships, within our communities and within our Movement. We resolve to make every effort to embrace holiness of life, knowing that this is only possible by means of the power of the Holy Spirit producing his fruit in us.

THE Army's tenth doctrine boldly declares: 'We believe that it is the privilege of all believers to be wholly sanctified, and that their whole spirit and soul and body may be preserved blameless till the coming of our Lord Jesus Christ.' The doctrine is a direct quotation from 1 Thessalonians 5:23.

In the Hebrew language, words used to describe the holiness of God speak of him as being 'set apart'. In the Greek New Testament the words *hagios* or *haggiasmos* have the same religious meaning: the separateness of God. There was no holiness apart from God. People or things only became holy when they participated in the life of God.

In the New Testament, Jesus Christ is presented as a model of the selfless and devoted life, and the work of Jesus and his Spirit are the means by which the Church and the individual are sanctified. Most of Paul's references to holiness or sanctification have a specific moral application.

Following Wesley's emphasis of the doctrine of holiness, William Booth made it a 'fundamental truth' of The Salvation Army. 'It stands in the front rank of our doctrines,' he said. 'We inscribe it upon our banners. Any officer who did not hold and proclaim the ability of Jesus Christ to save his people to the uttermost from sin and sinning, I should consider out of place amongst us' (1880).

Commissioner Samuel Logan Brengle wrote and preached prolifically on holiness. In 'The Holiness Standard of The Salvation Army' (which is included in Commissioner John Waldron's anthology *The Privilege of all Believers*) he wrote: 'It is this holiness – the doctrines, the experience, the action – that we Salvationists must maintain, else we shall betray our trust; we shall lose our birthright; we shall cease to be a spiritual power in the earth; we shall have a name to live and yet be dead; our glory will depart; and we, like Samson shorn of his locks, shall become as other men.' In this statement of belief in holy living there was a warning to recognise what could happen to the Army if holiness were to be neglected.

Brengle's prophetic words speak of the need for doctrine and experience to go hand in hand: 'Without the doctrine, the standard, the teaching, we shall never find the experience, or having found it, we shall be likely to lose it. Without the experience we shall neglect the teaching, we shall doubt or despise the doctrine, we shall lower the standard.'

The Army's holiness meetings have highlighted the integral part this doctrine has played in the lives of its soldiers through the years. In countries the world over, Sunday morning holiness meetings have marked the call to worship for Salvationists, but Brengle has more to say: 'When officers lose the experience, the holiness meetings languish, and when they languish, the spiritual life of the corps droops and falls, and all manner of substitutes and expedients are introduced to cover up the ghastly facts of spiritual loss, disease and death.'

Colonel Phil Needham reminds us that holiness encompasses all the attributes of God, including his love. 'A true holiness meeting is grounded in who God the Holy One is, and invites his people to respond to him by becoming like him, and living as his holy people in the world.' He continues: 'In the presence of God we see ourselves for who we really are and the values by which we live, for what they really are. There is no room for deception, no allowance for escapism. The holiness of God invites us to look honestly at our lives, to see where transformation is needed, and by his sanctifying grace actually to make those changes.'

The importance of teaching holiness is outlined in *Orders and Regulations for Officers of The Salvation Army (Volume II)*:

'It is the responsibility of an officer to teach holiness intelligently yet simply. He should not bewilder his people with theological terms which they cannot understand, but use every opportunity, as God shall help him, to lead them to yield their forgiven lives completely to the will of God so that his Spirit may possess them fully.'

To assist understanding of holiness, its nature and outworking, libraries of songs have been written. Countless Salvationists have best understood their holiness doctrine through songs. Major Cecil Waters (R), speaking at the William Booth Memorial Training College, London, reasoned: 'I suspect that *pro-rata* more Salvationists own a song book than do Christians of other persuasions their hymnaries. Our song book has long been seen as an essential aid to our devotion, and indeed our spiritual progress.'

Holiness songs have played a defining role in the life of Salvationists everywhere, some songs having been penned by Salvationists and some borrowed from other Christian poets. Charles Wesley's songs clearly and challengingly point us to the essence of holiness:

> *Thy nature, gracious Lord, impart,*
> *Come quickly from above;*
> *Write thy new name upon my heart,*
> *Thy new best name of love.*

General Frederick Coutts has described holiness as 'Christlikeness' – seeking to be like Christ, growing in him and he in us. In *Essentials of*

Christian Experience, he wrote: 'Christlikeness is holiness. Where Christ is enthroned, there is holiness. Yet holiness is never an "imitation" of Christ, if by that is meant a self-conscious external patterning. Christian holiness will spring from the inward possession of that same Holy Spirit who was in Jesus . . . The blessing of holiness is never an "it". No one should say: "I've got it!", for the experience is personal and the source of the experience is personal. . . The work of the Spirit was perfectly exemplified in Jesus and he can make us like him, not through any outward conformity but by the workings of inward grace.'

Salvationist songwriter Lieut-Colonel Colin Fairclough describes the hope as a prayer:

> *Christ of Glory, Prince of Peace,*
> *Let thy life in mine increase;*
> *Though I live may it be shown*
> *'Tis thy life and not my own.*
> *Dwell within, that men may see*
> *Christ, the living Christ, in me.*

Leslie Taylor-Hunt's much-used song reveals a prayer which has motivated so much selfless Salvation Army service:

> *Give me a holy life,*
>   *Spotless and free,*
> *Cleansed by the crystal flow*
>   *Coming from thee.*
> *Purge the dark halls of thought,*
> *Here let thy work be wrought,*
> *Each wish and feeling brought*
>   *Captive to thee.*

Through the years the terms 'sinless perfection' and 'Christian perfection' have been used to describe the holy life, not always with success and sometimes creating confusion. John Wesley went to great lengths at the 1759 Methodist Conference to define 'Christian perfection', which he read as being synonymous with 'entire sanctification' or 'holiness'. The stated definition was 'loving God with all our heart, mind, soul and strength'. It continued: 'This implies that no wrong temper, none contrary to love remains in the soul; and that all the thoughts, words, and actions are covered by pure love.'

In *Earthen Vessels* Lieut-Colonel Milton Agnew summed the matter up this way: 'Man's perfection lies not in accomplishment, but in spirit; not in performance, but in purpose. It is to Christian perfection that

God calls us, not to sinless perfection. Sinless perfection says that one is not able to sin. Christian perfection declares that he is able not to sin. And therein lies a world of difference. Sinless perfection would lift a person out of the world of reality, out of his normal human nature, out of a world of decision and responsibility. That God would never do. But the ability both to sin and not to sin puts upon the believer a challenging responsibility of choice, together with a divinely given provision.'

Helpful or unhelpful as definitions may be, the call to holiness in all its dimensions reminds us that the holy life necessarily involves personal, relational, social and political attitudes. The experience of holiness isn't merely a very blessed spiritual feeling on a Sunday morning. If it is anything at all, it has its outworking in everyday life, seven days a week. Holiness demands that we get our hands dirty while asking God to keep our hearts clean. It must make a defining difference as to how we live and to the people we are.

It shouldn't be overlooked that holiness is linked with wholeness and health. Writing in *Health, Healing and Wholeness*, Colonel Phil Needham says: 'If we, the Church, are to have a mission in the world that facilitates real healing, we must have a ministry to ourselves which brings us toward wholeness . . . In order to do this, we must pay attention to that which keeps the Church from health.'

Wholeness is an expression of holiness. In response to the example and command of Christ, and the presence and prompting of his Spirit, we are called to wholeness in all areas of life. We are called to so live that body, mind and soul are dedicated to God.

At the risk of stating the obvious, holiness of life does not occur by accident. This gracious gift is not received by those who fail to seek it, or by those who are casual about their own spirituality. Jesus told his disciples that those who 'hunger and thirst after righteousness' would be filled, not those who simply take what comes along. This is why the Commission looks to Salvationists everywhere to 'resolve to make every effort to embrace holiness of life, knowing that this is only possible by means of the power of the Holy Spirit producing his fruit in us'.

When research was undertaken among Salvationists to ascertain which aspects of our life together were felt to be integral to the life of the Army, holiness was emphasised again and again. Acceptance of a spiritual 'second best' is not worthy of Christ's followers. It doesn't work. It isn't satisfying.

Writing to the Romans, the apostle Paul urges his fellow-Christians to offer their bodies as living sacrifices 'holy and pleasing to God' (12:1). He warns against conforming to the pattern of the world and urges transformation by allowing God to renew our thinking. As the chapter proceeds he highlights some of the practical outworkings of the Christian life. It will not be easy. It will not necessarily come naturally. But it is the only way to ensure that evil is overcome. There is no sitting on the fence, no compromise. 'Do not be overcome by evil, but overcome evil with good' (v 21). Be holy!

Questions:

1.   What makes God's people holy?

2.   What are the personal practical implications of embracing holiness of life?

3.   What are the practical implications for our corps of embracing holiness of life?

4.   How can we ensure that holiness teaching is given its needful place in our corps?

Scripture to consider:

1 Thessalonians 5:23, 24, Romans 12:1-21,
Ephesians 1:4, Hebrews 12:10, 1 Peter 1:16.

Call to
War

We call Salvationists worldwide to join spiritual battle on the grounds of a sober reading of Scripture, a conviction of the triumph of Christ, the inviolable freedom and dignity of persons, and a commitment to the redemption of the world in all its dimensions – physical, spiritual, social, economic and political.

We affirm that Christ our Lord calls us to join him in holy war against evil in all its forms and against every power that stands against the reign of God. We fight in the power of the Spirit in the assurance of ultimate and absolute victory through Christ's redemptive work. We reject extreme attitudes towards the demonic: on the one hand, denial; on the other, obsession. We affirm that the body of Christ is equipped for warfare and service through the gifts of the Spirit. By these we are strengthened and empowered. We heed the injunction of Scripture to value all God's gifts, and rejoice in their diversity.

THE Salvation Army was born to battle. From its earliest days war on evil was declared. One month before The Christian Mission became The Salvation Army, William Booth spoke to a War Congress: 'We are sent to war,' he said. 'We are not sent to minister to a congregation and be content if we keep things going. We are sent to make war . . . and to stop short of nothing but the subjugation of the world to the sway of the Lord Jesus.'

Two days before, the Congress had been opened with the singing of a song which was subsequently to be used as a rallying cry around the world:

> Sound the battle cry!
>   See, the foe is nigh,
> Raise the standard high
>   For the Lord.
> Gird your armour on;
> Stand firm every one;
> Rest your cause upon
>   His holy word.

Not surprisingly, the Army's motives were sometimes misunderstood. But this war was not against people. The use of force was never considered. Far from it. This Army was designed to fight *for* people, to rescue them from poverty, misery, injustice and pain. The weapons required for this were spiritual and as such could be received only from God. By 1950 Colonel Catherine Baird had penned some words which have remained significant for their clarity:

> We're in God's Army and we fight
>   Wherever wrong is found;
> A lowly cot or stately home
>   May be our battle ground.
> We own no man as enemy,
>   Sin is our challenged foe;
> We follow Jesus, Son of God,
>   As to the war we go.
>
> When our invading forces march,
>   In every tongue we sing;
> We are of every class and race,
>   Yet one in Christ, the King.
> Our Master's darkest battlefield,
>   Upon a lonely height,
> Reveals God's sword to everyone,
>   A cross of love and light.

His Kingdom cometh not by force
    But, by the gentle power
Of righteousness and truth and grace,
    He triumphs every hour.
Sometimes his happy people march
    With banners floating high,
Though often in secluded ways,
    They fight that self may die.

The good fight is the fight of faith,
    Heaven's victories are won
By men unarmed, save with the mind
    That was in Christ, the Son.
As morning overwhelms the night,
    So truth shall sin o'erthrow,
And love at last shall vanquish hate
    As sunshine melts the snow.

Catherine Baird wrote the song, she said, 'in an effort to make clear that The Salvation Army is exactly opposite to the armies of violence'. She continued: 'To save, not to destroy, is our aim. And although we go to battle, it is not with men, but to overthrow by means of God's weapons of love and grace, the evil in the world.' This battle will always be central to the Army's mission.

Appropriately then, the Commission highlights the Lord's call to join him in holy war against evil in all its forms and against every power that stands against the reign of God. Salvationists are called to a commitment to the redemption of the world in all its dimensions – physical, spiritual, social, economic, political.

In recent years there has been increased interest in the subject of spiritual conflict, and terms and beliefs which once seemed clear and straightforward have taken on new meanings, or become the subject of fierce debate within the Church. When a working group of the Lausanne Committee for World Evangelisation met in the early 1990s it noted 'widespread concern about the reality of spiritual warfare with the powers of darkness' and listed what it saw as nine dangers and their antidotes:

1. There is a danger that we revert to think and operate on pagan worldviews or on an undiscerning application of Old Testament analogies that were in fact superseded in Jesus Christ. The antidote to this is the rigorous study of the whole of Scripture, always interpreting the Old Testament in the light of the New.

2. A preoccupation with the demonic can lead to avoiding personal responsibility for our actions. This is countered by equal emphasis on 'the world' and 'the flesh' and the strong ethical teachings of the Bible.

3. A preoccupation with the powers of darkness can exalt Satan and diminish Jesus in the focus of his people. This is cured by encouraging a Christ-centred and not an experience-centred spirituality of methodology.

4. The tendency to shift the emphasis to 'power' and away from 'truth' forgets that error, ignorance and deception can only be countered by biblical truth clearly and consistently taught. This is equally if not more important than tackling bondage and possession by 'power encounters'. It is also the truth that sets us free, so the Word and the Spirit need to be kept in balance.

5. We observed the tendency to emphasise technique and methodology in the practice of spiritual warfare and fear that, when this is dominant, it can become a substitute for the pursuit of holiness and even of evangelism itself. To combat this there is no substitute for a continuous strong, balanced and Spirit-guided teaching ministry in each church.

6. We had reports of growing disillusionment with the results of spiritual warfare in unrealised expectations, unmet predictions and the sense of being marginalised if the language and practice of spiritual warfare is not adopted and just general discomfort with too much triumphalist talk. The antidote to all of this is a return to the whole teaching of Jesus on prayer, especially what he says about praying in secret that avoids ostentation.

7. While recognising that someone initially has to go to a people to introduce the gospel, we felt it was necessary always for the encounter with the powers of darkness to be undertaken by Christian people within the culture and in a way that is sensitive in applying biblical truth to their context.

8. We are cautious about the way in which the concept of territorial spirits is being used, and look to our biblical scholars to shed more light on this recent development.

9. We heard with concern of situations where warfare language was pushing Christians into adversarial attitudes to people and where people of other faiths were interpreting this as the language of violence and political involvement. We saw that the language of peace, penitence and reconciliation must be as prominent in our speech and practice as any talk of warfare.

In *This Means War,* Major Chick Yuill brings his perceptions to the subject:

'There is little doubt that some writers on the subject of spiritual warfare have gone far further than Scripture itself in 'their concern to construct elaborate and detailed demonologies. It is also true that some people have opted out of personal responsibility, blaming their actions on the devil. But the case has, I think, been greatly overstated. A proper awareness of the demonic has very positive ethical effects on us. It makes it impossible for us to think that evil is "just one side of our nature"; it alerts us to the subtlety and persistence of temptation; and it reminds us more clearly than anything else that, since we are up against such powerful foes, we cannot succeed in the moral life without a complete reliance on the enabling grace of God.'

Lieut-Colonel Stuart Mungate, participating in the Commission's work from an African perspective, spoke of witch-doctor activity and spirit-world concepts which Westerners sometimes seem either reluctant or unable to grasp. Chick Yuill makes a further point: 'A city or a nation which has enjoyed centuries of Christian teaching and tradition will obviously be very different in character from a society whose customs and thought-patterns are rooted in and conditioned by pagan religion. Evangelism will be most effective where we understand the spiritual background and adapt the presentation of our message accordingly.'

Reflecting on the Lausanne Statement, Chick Yuill wrote: 'Nothing destroys the effectiveness of a fighting unit more quickly than when feuding breaks out amongst its own soldiers. Morale is quickly sapped and the army is open to the counter-attack of the enemy. We must not allow that to happen to the army of Jesus Christ. It would be particularly ironic if Christians were to be divided on the subject of spiritual warfare!'

Concern about concepts and understanding of spiritual warfare grew with the proliferation of evangelical groups which had failed or neglected to define their doctrine. This concern has been shared by Salvationists and when youth representatives from around the Army world met in South Africa in 1997 they also asked for clarification.

The Commission was able to consider the Lausanne Statement and appreciated why it had become necessary. Dr Roger Green pointed out: 'It is wrong to affirm an open dualism – that is to preach, teach or even imply that in the battle of good against evil only at the conclusion of history will we know which side wins the battle. The most serious error in this regard is made by Christians who ascribe to Satan the attributes of God, as though Satan were all-knowing, present everywhere, or all-powerful' (Matthew 12:29). He continued: 'However, both the Bible and experience teach us that, although the end of the story is clear, evil still battles against good. The Church is engaged in warfare against both personal and corporate sin. It is in warfare against the sins of injustice, prejudice and hatred, which enslave institutions as well as nations. For such spiritual warfare, God has equipped his Church with the gifts of the Spirit.'

The Commission sees it as vital to emphasise that Christians fight in the power of the Spirit in the assurance of ultimate and absolute victory through Christ's redemptive work. In John 16:33 Jesus tells his disciples: 'Be of good cheer, I have overcome the world.' The Master had no doubts about the victory. Neither should we.

Bearing this fully in mind, and being representative of various cultures, the Commission made the following emphasis: 'We reject extreme attitudes towards the demonic: on the one hand, denial; on the other, obsession. We affirm that the body of Christ is equipped for warfare and service through the gifts of the Spirit. By these we are strengthened and empowered.'

Back in the 1880s Catherine Booth saw the danger of becoming complacent: 'It is a bad sign for the Christianity of this day that it provokes so little opposition. If there were not other evidence of it being wrong, I should know it from that. When the Church and the world can jog along comfortably together you may be sure there is something wrong. The world has not altered. Its spirit is exactly the same as it ever was, and if Christians were equally faithful and devoted to the Lord and separated from the world, living so that their lives were a reproof to all ungodliness, the world would hate them as much as it ever did.'

In recognising the Army's victories over evil through the years, Roger Green also points out that 'some urgent battles are not being fought – such as, unjust legislation, racism, failure to distribute wealth among those who are most in need, remaining silent against the powers who defy the authority of the Church'. The call to ensure that these and other battles are fought is not only for those who lead the Army at corps, divisional or territorial level, but also for every Salvationist to play his or her part to make the world a better place, by the Spirit's power.

The apostle Paul has left in Scripture words of guidance, challenge and reassurance. In Ephesians 6:12 he writes passionately of the battle 'against the powers of this dark world and against the spiritual forces of evil in the heavenly realms'. He then lists the armour needed for Christians to fight in the 'mighty power' of the Lord.

In Romans 8 he puts the opposition in its place! For those who may still be haunted by past wrongdoing, weakened by fear, he boldly declares: 'There is now no condemnation for those who are in Christ Jesus, because through Christ Jesus the law of the Spirit of life set me free from the law of sin and death' (v 1). Christians who are fooled or tricked into thinking that their past sins can condemn them are reassured that this is not so. They must not allow the fight to be taken out of them. Later in the same chapter (v 31) Paul, by means of a question, shows the power of God's foes for what it is. 'If God is for us, who can be against us?' God is all-powerful. No foe can match him.

In other parts of Scripture there are frequent references to 'fear'. In Psalm 23 the psalmist says he will 'fear no evil' because God is with him. Psalm 34:9 says: 'Fear the Lord, you his saints, for those who fear him lack nothing.' Psalm 47:2 reminds us that 'the Lord, the Most High, is to be feared'. Reference after reference points to an appropriate fear of the Lord. Significantly, *nowhere in Scripture are we told to fear the devil.*

In James 4:7 we are urged to 'resist the devil' with the promise that he will then flee from us. In 1 Peter 5:8 we are reminded that our enemy the devil 'prowls around like a roaring lion looking for someone to devour'. Again we are urged to resist him. But there is no advice to fear him. Although we must not be careless, flippant, unguarded or foolishly dismissive of the devil, we need never fear him. Neither should we attribute to him things which he does not have the power to accomplish. To be deceived into a fear of the devil undermines our spiritual effectiveness. Paul will have none of it. 'Who shall separate us from the love of Christ?' he asks. 'Shall trouble or hardship or persecution or famine or nakedness or danger or sword? . . . No, in all these things we are more than conquerors through him who loved us' (Romans 8:37). Whatever our human difficulty, Christ is with us.

Paul then moves on to the spiritual world. His message is unequivocal. 'For I am convinced that neither death nor life, neither angels nor demons, neither the present nor the future, nor any powers, neither height nor depth, nor anything else in all creation, will be able to separate us from the love of God that is in Christ Jesus our Lord' (v 38, 39).

Such confidence is at the heart of our faith. It is founded on the power of the Christ who has conquered the world. We are urged to claim it, to live by it, to prove it.

Questions:

1. When Jesus said, 'Be of good cheer, I have overcome the world', what was he telling us?

2. How committed are we to fighting evil in all its forms?

3. How awake are we to the spiritual needs around us?

4. What kind of Holy Spirit resources do we need to be effective for Christ?

Scripture to consider:

John 16:33, Ephesians 3:20, 21 and 6:10-18,
Romans 8:1, 2, 9-11, 31-39 and 16:20,
1 John 5:5.

Call
to the Family

We call Salvationists worldwide to restore the family to its central position in passing on the faith, to generate resources to help parents grow together in faithful love and to lead their children into wholeness, with hearts on fire for God and his mission.

We affirm that the family plays a central role in passing on the faith. We also recognise that families everywhere are subject to dysfunction and disintegration in an increasingly urbanised world in which depersonalisation, insignificance, loneliness and alienation are widespread. We believe that in the home where Christ's Lordship is acknowledged, and the family is trained in God's word, a spiritually enriching and strengthening environment is provided.

'THE family faces inward to the individual and outward to society. It has enormous potential, including that of life itself, and it is not surprising that, when it becomes disordered, it possesses an equal potential for terrible destruction.' These words of psychiatrist-scholar Dr Robin Skynner remind us that to ignore the family and its needs is to invite trouble.

Families function in different ways throughout the world. Cultures determine attitudes, and lifestyles dictate closeness or otherwise. Since the Second World War the Western world has seen enormous social changes which have affected family life in many ways. Various factors have been at work in changing the social structure and functioning of households and families.

There has been a general decline in the birth rate. Improved health standards have contributed to a vast increase in the proportion of elderly people in society. Yet the elderly stand in danger of being seen as a problem rather than as a resource of wisdom and experience.

The liberalisation of laws on abortion and the availability of contraception have resulted in more children being born outside marriage in countries which previously had strongly-held views on the essential place of marriage within society. The proportion of couples living together rather than marrying is rising in almost every Western country. In the United Kingdom more than half the babies born are conceived out of wedlock.

In countries where marriage is still popular, frequently the divorce rate is also seen to be growing. Liberal divorce laws have made legal termination of marriages easier. The number of children affected by divorce continues to grow, with figures varying from country to country.

Not unnaturally, the number of second marriages has increased and this has led to the formation of many step-families.

With a worldwide boom in immigration during the past 50 years, the number of mixed marriages has increased and the sharing of different family systems has developed.

A greater regard for the role of women has been significant too. Most children now have both parents working and this has had an effect on the way each household functions.

The introduction of new forms of technology, increased mobility and an explosion in the influence and impact of the media have affected social relationships at all levels. Parents or their children 'lose themselves' in their computers; many couples have separate employment, separate cars and separate lives. The media (television, newspapers and magazines) has its effect on all members of the family, particularly children, and this can result in influences outside the home having the major effect on the lives of younger members of the family.

The impact of organised religion has steadily declined and this has changed people's perceptions of the way they should live. Frequently they have no knowledge of Scripture or understanding of Christian ethics. There is a 'new morality' which makes up its own mind.

There has been a growing acceptance and tolerance of alternative sexual lifestyles. The right to choose how to express one's sexuality has caused confusion both within and outside the Church.

Not every country has been affected to the same degree by these changes, but in the global village the impact of the disintegration of family life has had, and is having, a far-reaching effect.

Yet the family remains a symbol of hope in our world. It is the basic regenerative and nurturing unit of society. It is the family that inspires commitment to meeting human need at all stages of life; the care, education, and development of children, the support of the sick and disabled and the elderly.

Dr Martin Luther King said: 'Family life not only educates in general, but its quality ultimately determines the individual's capacity to love. The institution of the family is decisive in determining not only if a person has the capacity to love another individual, but in the larger social sense, whether he is capable of loving his fellow men collectively. The whole of society rests on this foundation, for stability, understanding and social peace.'

The Salvation Army has always seen, understood and promoted the value of the family. Throughout the centuries the family has held a central position in passing on religious faith, Christian or otherwise. Some traditions still achieve this with remarkable success in a pluralistic society. Yet many modern families fail to share a meal together once a week, let alone once a day. Meals provide opportunity to meet, to have conversation, to share in each other's lives and to talk about the events of the day. A great proportion of the population are likely to hear more words within their home from the television or radio than from another family member.

Opportunities for shared prayer seem to be rare. Family members leave home at different times – children for school, father to the office, mother often leaving slightly later for other employment. They return at different times. They then have other duties, such as homework, household chores, or friends to meet. Some families cope remarkably well with the rush and tear of modern society. They somehow let each other know that they are valued, loved and supported. Other families just fall apart, gradually or swiftly.

The Commission calls on Salvationists worldwide to acknowledge the seriousness of the situation and, as far as possible, to restore the family to its central position in life, especially in passing on the faith. This can be achieved, but a determined effort is required. Grace at meal times, family prayers, shared worship on Sundays and a social life based within a Christian fellowship all have a positive influence.

But with attacks on the value of family life increasing, families need to be aware of both subtle and not so subtle dangers, and to guard against them. This is one reason why the Commission is encouraging the provision of resources to help parents grow together in faithful love, and lead their children into wholeness and holiness, with hearts on fire for God and his mission.

Parents need help. When the first child arrives each parent is usually aware of his or her own inadequacy. Parenthood is new. Parents practice as they go along. They know the experience is new. In recent years the Army has produced more books, guidelines and preparation classes for people approaching marriage. These resources encourage faithful love and understanding of each other's needs.

Families need fidelity and commitment from husband and wife if they are to survive and function successfully. It has been said that the best gift parents can give to their children is to love each other. Children learn from example and gain personal security in a stable environment.

It is also recognised that where families are subject to dysfunction and disintegration in an increasingly urbanised world, depersonalisation, insignificance, loneliness and alienation have become widespread. A higher degree of commitment is required if those who have become marginalised by society are to find their place again within society and the family of God. To discover and accept that there is a place within the fellowship of believers requires a strong support system. Those who have been marginalised or who have lost confidence have a contribution to make to each fellowship, but they first need to be assured that there is a place for them.

The Salvation Army is frequently complimented on its social services and community work. Those having a tough time in life can be put back on their feet by the Army's service and ministry, but the question as to how adequately each corps ministers to the needs of people who feel depersonalised, lonely, insignificant or alienated may be a very different matter.

The structure for achieving this is not so easy to put into place or into operation. As has been acknowledged before, corps can become exclusive, even without realising it. Any corps looking at this subject could be surprised and then revitalised in its ministry when it discovers what opportunities are waiting to be grasped. The Call is in effect for every corps to show it is part of the all-embracing family of God.

Questions:

1. In what ways do we give quality time to the essential needs (physical and spiritual) of our families?

2. How can families be helped to identify with faithful love and holy living?

3. How adequately is our corps ministering to the needs of people who feel depersonalised, lonely, insignificant or alienated?

4. How does our corps reflect in practice the family of God?

Scripture to consider:

Mark 10:13-16, Galatians 6:10, 1 Timothy 3:1-13,
James 2:14-18, 1 John 3:16-20 and 5:1-4, 3 John 4,
Ephesians 3:14-19.

The Sacraments

An Explanation

At the conclusion of the Commission's consultations, statements on Holy Communion and baptism were formulated. The wording of both statements was unanimously agreed. Also presented, to give insight into some of the reasoning behind the statements, was a rationale on the statement on Holy Communion. This rationale can only begin to reflect the deep and far-reaching considerations given. A book in its own right would be needed to cover the subject adequately.

It may be helpful to point out that before the Commission arrived at its statements with their 10 clearly defined points, and before the rationale was agreed, members of the Commission engaged in much prayer (personal and corporate), read masses of correspondence, shared Bible studies, felt the benefit of opinions from other churches and eventually looked at 10 questions which were given personal and private consideration. The 10 questions are listed below. When Commission members brought their answers to the group to share them, all did so verbally and were then given opportunity to explain their reasons. Everyone – not just those who might normally be most ready to debate – was given equal opportunity to express his or her point of view and convictions.

1. Do you believe that the receiving of the grace of God is not dependent upon any particular ceremony or ritual?

2. Do you believe that the sacrament of Holy Communion should be introduced (in some form) in Salvation Army worship?

3. Is it practical to think in terms of its introduction?

4. Do you believe that unless the sacrament of Holy Communion is practised by the Army, we are being disobedient to the Lord Jesus Christ?

5. Do you believe that water baptism should be introduced into the Army?

6. Is it practical to think in terms of its introduction? (Please comment on perceived difficulties and how they could be overcome.)

7. Acknowledging that we believe Salvationists are baptised into Christ through the indwelling of the Holy Spirit, would you support the inclusion of words to this effect in the swearing-in ceremony? (No water required.)

8. Do you think there is room for exploring a fellowship meal style of worship?

9. Would you favour a re-emphasis of the love feast?

10. If introduced, should fellowship meals or love feasts contain specific (ceremonial) words?

It should also be noted here that, as the statement on Holy Communion reminds us, terminology (such as 'love feast') varies according to culture and denomination, and is not always interchangeable. Although it is not possible to share adequately the complexities which this brings to such a debate, questions raised in the paper presented by Colonel Shaw Clifton (included in this section) define some of the issues which were addressed. The earlier chapter 'Call to Celebrate Christ's Presence' also has a strong link with this section.

In its Statement on baptism, the Commission acknowledges that 'there are many worthy ways of publicly witnessing to having been baptised into Christ's body by the Holy Spirit'. It also recognises that water baptism, practised by some other Christians, is among them.

The Salvation Army has no dispute with denominations who use water baptism as an initiation right for believers into the Church. *One Faith One Church* (The Salvation Army's response to the World Council of Churches' Faith and Order Paper No. 111) says: 'With Christians who observe the sacrament of water baptism in deep spiritual understanding, Salvationists have true fellowship in spirit.'

Water baptism, however, has never been part of Salvation Army practice. The Salvationist's position on baptism has been based on the belief that the only distinctive and utterly unique Christian baptism is baptism with the Holy Spirit (1 Corinthians 12:13; Ephesians 4:5). This cannot be duplicated by any other religion. It is peculiarly Christ's. As John declared by the Jordan river: 'I baptise you with water, but he (Jesus) will baptise you with the Holy Spirit' (Mark 1:8). The words of Jesus to his disciples prior to his Ascension show his priority: 'John baptised with water, but in a few days you will be baptised with the Holy Spirit' (Act 1:5). The Commission unitedly reaffirmed this emphasis and the Statement on baptism confirms this.

Yet the Commission also acknowledges that in certain parts of the world, according to culture, the Army's non-observance of the

Sacraments of Holy Communion and water baptism is sometimes not understood. Lack of understanding of the Army's position produces hindrances to the Army's growth and effectiveness. Some of the hindrances include:

- New converts lost to other churches.

- Discrimination within the body of Christ to which we rightly belong in partnership with other brothers and sisters.

- The continual need to explain the Army's perceived 'sacramental' but not 'sacramentalist' position.

- Belonging ethnically to people who think, live, act, work and worship, not so much with the mind but more with the heart.

- In areas where Christianity is already a minority, being seen as a minority within that minority.

These and other difficulties were given thorough consideration by the Commission, though it was overwhelmingly agreed not to recommend the introduction of water baptism. Its introduction would add nothing to the validity of Christian experience already enjoyed and, in the context of being introduced, could detract from the all-important baptism – that of the Spirit.

Non-Salvationist friends also helped with deliberations. In response to a question from a member, Bishop (Dr) John Austin Baker said he felt that it would be wrong ('a disaster') for the Army to introduce the Sacraments just to conform to what other churches were doing. The Army could lose its distinctive witness to the rest of the Church if it tried to be 'just like other churches'.

The minutes of the meeting also record the bishop as suggesting that the Army 'together with other churches, should express its common ground more clearly. Many churches would not realise that Salvationists regard themselves as being baptised, having received the gift of the Holy Spirit.'

The Commission later recommended the inclusion of words to this effect in the soldier's swearing-in ceremony and steps have already been taken to introduce appropriate wording. There was never any suggestion by the Commission that the baptism of infants should be part of Salvation Army practice.

COMMUNION

A Statement on Holy Communion

After full and careful consideration of The Salvation Army's understanding of, and approach to, the sacrament of Holy Communion*, the International Spiritual Life Commission sets out the following points:

1 God's grace is freely and readily accessible to all people at all times and in all places.

2 No particular outward observance is necessary to inward grace.

3 The Salvation Army believes that unity of the Spirit exists within diversity and rejoices in the freedom of the Spirit in expressions of worship.

4 When Salvationists attend other Christian gatherings in which a form of Holy Communion is included, they may partake if they choose to do so and if the host church allows.

5 Christ is the one true sacrament, and sacramental living – Christ living in us and through us – is at the heart of Christian holiness and discipleship.

6 Throughout its history The Salvation Army has kept Christ's atoning sacrifice at the centre of its corporate worship.

7 The Salvation Army rejoices in its freedom to celebrate Christ's real presence at all meals and in all meetings, and in its opportunity to explore in life together the significance of the simple meals shared by Jesus and his friends and by the first Christians.

8 Salvationists are encouraged to use the love feast and develop creative means of hallowing meals in home and corps with remembrance of the Lord's sacrificial love.

9 The Salvation Army encourages the development of resources for such events, which will vary according to culture, without ritualising particular words or actions.

10 In accordance with normal Salvation Army practice, such remembrances and celebrations, where observed, will not become established rituals, nor will frequency be prescribed.

* Terminology varies according to culture and denomination, and is not always interchangeable

Rationale on the Sacraments

The International Spiritual Life Commission engaged in an extensive discussion of the Army's position regarding the Sacraments. The process was probably the deepest, broadest and most extended in the history of our Movement. The theological depth of the discussion was secured by the presentation of papers by members of the Commission, both sitting and corresponding, which explored the Army's position from a scriptural, doctrinal and historical perspective.

Numerous publications, dissertations and papers received from Salvationists around the world contributed to the discussion. Scholars such as Bishop Lesslie Newbigin and Dr Nigel Wright contributed to the discussion by reading and commenting on key material. Bishop (Dr) John Austin Baker read some of the key papers and presented a paper of his own in response to the Commission. The breadth of the discussion was secured by the international membership of the Commission and the hundreds of submissions received from around the world which reflected the varying cultural context in which Salvationists engage in mission and the diversity of Salvationists' opinion worldwide.

The discussions were as extended in time as was necessary to secure an understanding of the concepts being shared. Members of the Commission sought to reach a common understanding, anticipating in faith the active guidance of the Holy Spirit, but without seeking to artificially produce agreement or to curtail a vigorous discussion in order to force a single view.

The Roman Catholic Church recognises seven sacraments: the baptism of infants and converts, the confirmation of baptism by the bishop, the rite of penitence and forgiveness, the anointing of the sick, the ordaining of priests, the uniting of people in marriage, and the Eucharist liturgy or mass.

Churches following in the Protestant tradition have tended to recognise only two sacraments. Luther wrote: 'There are, strictly speaking, but two sacraments in the Church of God – baptism and the bread.'

If the word 'sacrament' is understood in this sense, the Army, by its non-practice of baptism and the breaking of bread, is non-sacramental.

However, another broader definition has been applied in both ancient and modern times. St Augustine offered two famous definitions of 'sacrament': 'a sign of something sacred' and 'a visible sign of an invisible grace'. Salvationists do indeed have their own 'signs of something sacred' and some of our symbols, such as the flag and the mercy seat, could be described as 'visible signs of an invisible grace'. More recently Joseph Martos has explained that 'any ritual or object, person or place can be considered sacramental if it is taken to be a symbol of something that is sacred or mysterious'. By these definitions, ancient and modern, the Army is a sacramental Movement. We do not deny the value of the symbolic in religion.

However, we do not accept that tradition has a determining role in the formation of doctrine. We affirm of the Scriptures of the Old and New Testament that they only constitute the divine rule of Christian faith and practice.

The word 'sacrament' is not found in the Old or New Testaments, there is no evidence of a concept, such as the sacramental, which draws together baptism and the breaking of bread under one head. When further investigation is undertaken into the origin and derivation of the word 'sacrament' then the following emerges:

'Sacrament' derives from the Latin *sacramentum*. *Sacramentum* was the word used in the Vulgate to translate the Greek *mysterion*. *Mysterion* is never applied to baptism nor the breaking of bread. It is used definitively by Paul in Colossians. In Colossians 2:2 the *mysterion* of God, Paul says, 'is Christ'; in Colossians 1:27 Paul says the *mysterion* is 'Christ in you, the hope of glory'.

Paul used the word *mysterion* in order to contrast the secret rituals of the Hellenistic mystery religions, which created in the worshipper a sense of the transcendent and divine, with the mystery at the heart of the Christian faith which is 'Christ in you, the hope of glory'.

However, by the end of the second century, writers such as Tertullian were using the religious context of *mysterion* and *sacramentum* in order to compare the rituals of the Church – baptism and the breaking of bread – with the rituals of other religions, and to support the claim that the pagan mysteries were imitations or anticipations of the Christian mysteries.

In this way *mysterion* and *sacramentum* came to lose their radical New Testament meaning and gained a meaning deriving from the mystery cults. It came to be that '*mysterion* = re-presentation of the cultic deity = means of grace'.

The New Testament does not offer a mediation of grace through things, but through persons. 'Christ in you' speaks of a radical immediacy of grace, mediated through the persons of the Son of God and the Spirit of God to the Church and to the believer.

Such insights offer the possibility of another understanding of the term 'sacramental'. As Christ within is revealed in the outward as well as the inner life of the believer, so the believer mediates Christ to the world. The life of the believer might therefore be described as 'sacramental'. However, the New Testament does not speak in this way. The language of sacrament, as with the language of incarnation, is reserved for Christ alone, and is one of the many ways in which his uniqueness is affirmed. The New Testament uses the language of holiness and sanctification when speaking of the Christ-life lived out in the world.

Most contemporary scholarship supports this analysis of the New Testament evidence. This is why theologians such as the Catholic Edward Schillebeeckx and the Protestant Karl Barth speak of Christ as 'the sacrament of the encounter with God' or the 'primal sacrament'.

Many Christians share this view. They gladly affirm Christ as the one true sacrament of God. They gladly accept the reality of the immediacy of grace. However, they claim that obedience to the word of Christ requires Christians to baptise and break bread together. These acts have the status of ordinances. Christians should practice them because Christ commanded them.

Salvationists are bound in obedience to Christ, and our response to such a claim must be, 'What, then, does Christ require of us?'

For many Christians obedience to Christ's word found in Luke 22:19 and 1 Corinthians 11:24, to eat and drink in remembrance of his death, is fulfilled by participation in a symbolic meal held in the setting of the church in worship. However, there is evidence that the Church at first expressed its obedience to this command through participation in an ordinary shared meal.

Salvationists have the freedom to explore the many ways in which obedience to this command can be expressed. As they share meals with their families and their friends and within the fellowship of the Church, in ordinary meals or in simple symbolic meals, such as the love feast, they are able to remember the saving acts of Christ, to celebrate their participation in the fellowship of God's people and to anticipate the heavenly feast.

Some Christians express their obedience to Christ's words found in Matthew 28:18, 20 by the practice of infant baptism, others by baptising believers. These verses do not first and foremost constitute a command to baptise. The emphasis lies in the command to 'make disciples' and in the name of the triune God. However, the act of baptism forms a significant part of the process by which the Church fulfils Christ's great commission. Christ requires of his Church an action which reciprocates the Spirit's action in incorporating the believer into the body of Christ, that is the Church, and which stands as a witness by the individual believer to his or her new status in Christ.

The public swearing-in of a new soldier beneath the Trinitarian sign of the Army's tricolour flag is the means by which the Army recognises a new disciple and ushers him or her into the community of faith by means of an act of commitment to Christ and his mission. This is the means by which Salvationists express their obedience to the command of Christ found in the great commission.

William Booth's statement to Salvationists announcing our discontinuation of the Lord's Supper was not intended to stand for all time. He indicated the matter could be revisited in future. The Commission has done so, with the result that it is not thought necessary or appropriate to re-introduce the practise of sacramental observances at this time. However, as the Founder's statement was provisional, we believe that this provisionality should remain in place, and is an expression of the freedom of Salvationists to continue to respond in constant and instant obedience to the light the Holy Spirit sheds upon the word of God.

Our position as Salvationists is a position of freedom. The response of Salvationists worldwide to their freedom in Christ may be diverse, differing with the cultural context of indigenous Salvationist mission. Such freedom and diversity are to be prized as part of our heritage as Salvationists.

We have not always claimed that soldiership in the Army is synonymous with discipleship and membership of the Church and that the swearing-in of soldiers is effectively a response to the command to baptise believers. The Commission therefore recommends that the nature and requirements of soldiership and other forms of membership of the Army receive further consideration in the light of this claim.

Thinking aloud and candidly about The Salvation Army and the Sacraments

Part of a presentation by Colonel Shaw Clifton

(The publication of part of this presentation gives an indication of some of the issues which were considered.)

What has been said

A few examples of what has been said in Army literature on the Sacraments:

(a) William Booth's 17 January 1883 article in *The War Cry*, being his New Year address to officers, stresses that no sacrament can rightly be seen as a condition of salvation. He then speaks about sacraments and the need for the Army to avoid the 'grave dissension' sometimes associated with them. These are given as his reason for not issuing some formal directive to Salvationists. He wants each individual Salvationist to follow their own conscience but adds, 'In our own ranks let us be united, and go our own way.'

(b) In an earlier *War Cry* article on 4 November 1882, Booth had urged a gathering of the majors of the Army never to attempt satire on sacraments; to avoid taking Salvationists to churches if a sacrament were to be held there; and to march out of churches where the sermon was about sacraments.

(c) In 1945 The Salvation Army published a booklet *Salvationists and the Sacraments* and reprinted this in 1954. It begins with an extract from Minnie Lindsay Carpenter's *Life of William Booth*. She refers to Booth facing up to the question of sacraments when 'The Salvation Army became definitely, and with every sign of permanence, a branch of the Christian Church'.

She mentions the Quaker influences upon our Founders and the position taken by the Society of Friends, that the inner experience of grace could be and was real without the ritual externals. Booth, she wrote, 'pointed his people to the privilege and necessity of seeking the substance rather than the shadow'.

In place of infant baptism, he introduced the dedicating of infants to God. In place of adult baptism, he introduced soldiership and swearing-in under the flag. Neither of those was seen as a sacrament in the traditional sense, but came quickly to be seen as a means of grace.

In place of the Lord's Supper, he called upon his soldiers to let their daily lives be a continual recognition of their union with Christ, and to let every meal be a remembrance of Christ's death. Here were the seeds of Salvationist sacramentalism free from rituals.

(d) William Metcalf's *The Salvationist and the Sacraments* was published in 1965. In this he offered some warnings:

● About the danger of having any ceremony (sacramental or otherwise) 'which we repeat over and over again because we worship God in it'. (This is the sense in which I use the term 'ritual', in this paper.)

● About forgetting that the Army is part of the prophetic tradition which from Old Testament times has declared against all comers that ceremonial religion is not the only way to God.

● About losing our composure and our nerve when faced with the loneliness (either individually or as a group) that obeying God in our prophetic role can bring about.

(e) Another book is Major Clifford Kew's *Closer Communion* published in 1980. In his final chapter he points out that our position on sacraments 'did not originate in any ingrained prejudice against them, nor from any desire just to be different'. Rather, it was all a gradual process due to:

● Practical difficulties; and

● Growing convictions.

We need to ask, with the utmost care, whether these practical factors and these theological convictions have ceased either to apply or to be valid. It is, therefore, important to refer to factors such as:

● A healthy awareness of the risks of ritualism.

● Our conviction that there is no scriptural basis for regarding any sacramental ritual as essential to salvation.

- The often divisive influence which sacramental doctrines and practices have had upon the churches.

- The linking, in some Christian traditions, of sacraments to an exclusive few who may administer them.

- The position and ministry of women.

- The evidence of the holy lives of the Quakers who, in many parts of the world, practised no sacraments.

Major Kew offers four quotations to round off his analysis:

(i) A reporter in India: 'The Salvationists never for a moment lay aside their consciousness that they are in the immediate presence of the Deity. They never quit it. They are as close to his feet while singing a song, beating a drum, or talking to a crowd, as when prostrate in prayer.'

(ii) Professor John McQuarrie (*Principles of Christian Theology*): 'Although The Salvation Army has no sacraments, we could not for a moment deny that it receives and transmits divine grace.'

(iii) Paul to the Colossians (2:16, 17, *NEB*): 'Allow no one therefore to take you to task about what you eat or drink, or over the observance of festival, new moon or Sabbath. These are no more than a shadow of what was to come; the solid reality is Christ's.'

(iv) William Booth at Exeter Hall meeting on 13 March 1889: 'Neither water, sacraments, church services nor Salvation Army methods will save you without a living, inward change of heart and a living, active faith and communion with God . . .'

(f) In a December 1993 issue of *Salvationist* the then Major Raymond Caddy, in response to views expressed in the 'Letters' column, presented an authoritative article in which he recognised the Army's stance as a 'vital testimony to the efficacy of grace mediated by Christ'. He did not wish to 'exchange our birthright for a ceremonial that has constantly caused differences among Christians'. Carefully note his use of the word 'birthright'.

(g) Colonel Philip Needham in his *Community in Mission*, published by IHQ in 1987, speaks of Army social service as 'the sacrament of the Good Samaritan'. He goes on to say: 'This is the sacrament of the Church in mission, the sacrament in which the healing, reconciling grace of God becomes incarnate as a servant dresses the wounds of one who is otherwise looked upon as an enemy. It is an open sign . . . It is both a feat and a feast . . . it actually implies the new life in Christ.'

We are sacramentalists who do not practise any of the sacramental rituals commonly found, historically or currently, in other churches.

Captain John Read, in a paper presented to the International Spiritual Life Commission entitled *Closer Communion? The Salvationist and the Sacraments*, makes a centrally important point when he says: 'The alternative to the Sacraments for William Booth was certainly not an alternative set of symbols and traditions. The alternative was freedom. Yes, freedom from rituals, seen by others as essential either to salvation or ecclesiastical respectability, but not freedom from the underlying idea of sacramentalism itself, namely that God can and does reach to us, and through us to others, by means of all kinds of avenues, some formal and some informal. Even life itself, and our lives lived out for him, are so used to bless, and to cheer, and to build up, and to mediate God's grace.'

Let me attempt to summarise these sources. Several things strike me as I read them:

1 Not one of them rejects the idea of sacramentalism *per se*.

2 They all reject the idea that sacramentalist rituals are essential to anything at all.

3 They all see the Army as called to witness, or to testify, to the whole Church concerning the immediate and direct accessibility of God's grace apart from any particular ritual.

4 Some speak of our prophetic calling in this regard, a lonely calling.

5 Some see a clear connection between the Sacraments issue and our doctrine of the holy life. I will return to this later for I see it as a pivotal factor in what appears to be going on among us in the Army today.

What is going on?

Here are my personal perceptions of the present mood in the Army on sacraments:

(a) The disquiet expressed over sacraments is not new. It is not an exclusively modern phenomenon. I have been aware of it all my officership and even before that as a corps cadet and young local officer in the United Kingdom.

(b) The disquiet is often overstated. Dissenters are usually more vocal than conformists and this can give a false impression. I do not wish to be dismissive of the voices raised which ask for change. However, as a divisional commander for five years, and on two continents, I have met only one officer under my command who saw sacraments as an issue. He seemed to carry a sense of ecclesiastical inferiority which he (mistakenly in my view) thought would be cured by a change in our position on sacramental ritual. He felt it would change the attitudes of other ministers towards him and the Army. All this arose because he felt they looked down on him. I do not know if this tells us more about the other ministers or about my brother-officer.

(c) I sense distress among some Salvationists calling for change. They are distressed, for example, by such things as:

● A perceived lack of depth and a perceived absence of spiritual food in worship where they are; or

● A nagging doubt that we are disobeying words of Jesus; or

● A vague sense that without sacramental ritual we cannot be a genuine church or denomination; or

● Lack of numbers in our citadels and halls; or

● Difficulty in holding on to new converts and discipling them, especially those in cultures saturated by Roman Catholicism; or

● A feeling that other churches look down on us due to our position.

There appears to be a sense that all is not well with the Army and a minority has reached a diagnoses that the disease is called 'The

99

Absence of Sacramental Ritual'. If this is the diagnosis, the cure is said to be easy: 'The Inclusion of Sacramental Ritual'.

(d) I agree we have a disease. This is a generalisation, I know, but let us use it as a working hypothesis even at the risk of overstatement. The symptoms of the disease are seen in the Western world in such things as:

● Declining Sunday attendances in many places;

● Declining membership rolls in many places; and

● Smaller and smaller numbers entering officer training in many places.

Happily, there are many bright spots where the reverse is true, but let me stay within the broad generalisation for now, as it applies in the Western world.

I do not understand why it is thought that suddenly introducing the traditional sacramental rituals to our ways of worship will make the disease go away, or why doing so would address adequately or effectively any of the reasons for distress listed earlier in (c) above. The connection between our illness and the absence or otherwise of sacramental ritual has, frankly, yet to be demonstrated.

(e) We are, I believe, witnessing a misdiagnosis of our ills, and so the cure proposed cannot work. I have made it very clear that I believe we are, to varying degrees, ill in some key parts of the Army body. But the illness cannot rightly be called 'The Absence of Sacramental Ritual'. If I had to name it, I would instead call it 'Disobedience to God'. I am referring to a very specific disobedience which set in almost imperceptibly generations ago and which is still with us. Let me try to be clearer, even if I again indulge in generalisations.

God called the Army into being to be faithful in a two-fold mission, a 'twin' mission. I refer here *not* to:

● Evangelism; and

● Social Service.

I stress this because one often hears these stated as our two-fold mission or our *raison d'être*.

The two-fold mission I have in mind is:

● The proclamation of salvation and the raising up of saved persons to be pro-active soul-winners; and

- The proclamation, teaching, and living out in practical example, of the life of holiness.

'Salvation' and 'Holiness' are our banners. They are meant to fly over every programme that we undertake for God. Our present illness, if a diagnosis be sought, is our disobedience concerning the second limb of our sacred calling, as an Army of Jesus.

So, it is not ritual that we lack, but holiness. It is not ritual that will cure us, but obedience to our first calling. It is not novelty that we need, but rediscovery of the things that once we knew, believed, taught, and to which we testified.

My pulse still races when I read again Brengle's prophetic words: 'Without the doctrine, the standard, the teaching, we shall never find the experience, or, having found it, we shall be likely to lose it. Without the experience we shall neglect the teaching, we shall doubt or despise the doctrine, we shall lower the standard.'

Brengle's voice reaches us across the decades. Were he among us today, he would tell us to urge the Army everywhere to guard against the pursuit of novelty, to refocus on first things, to go back to the old wells (even if the water containers might have a new look), and to recognise the cry for sacramental ritual for what it really is – a quest for a substitute, an expedient 'to cover up the ghastly facts of spiritual loss, disease and death'.

What is being asked for?

Any serious proposal for change in our attitude on sacramental matters would have to deal with at least the following:

- The reasons for Salvationists suddenly abandoning God's ways and dealings with them through the years.

- The reasons for supposing that God has now spoken plainly by his Spirit to the Army and has told us he is releasing us from our calling to be a witness to the truths set down clearly by Army writers and leaders through the years.

- The reasons for supposing that, if the Army is thus absolved by God from this task, the Church, as a whole, has moved beyond any need for such a counter-balancing witness (for no other group or denomination, even the Quakers, is as firm and clear about this as the Army and no other group is ready to assume our prophetic mantle).

101

- It must make practical suggestions for both the words and the means to explain to every Salvationist in the world why God's Army will now strike off at a sharp tangent from the ways in which God has hitherto led us.

- It must offer clear teaching about what the Army thinks a sacrament is, with equally clear teaching about what we think a sacrament is not.

- It must include clear exposition of *how many* sacraments the Army will now observe, with clear reasons as to why we are not going to hold rituals for all those sacraments which are regularly observed by other churches. Will we observe the seven Roman Catholic sacraments? If not, why not? If only some of these, why so? Will we observe rituals only for those sacraments called Dominical, that is, claimed to have been instituted by Jesus: baptism and the Lord's Supper? If only these, why only these, when for generations the Army has said to all the world that the evidence to support a claim for Christly institution is slim at best?

- If we embrace the rituals, what forms will we allow? For baptism, will we immerse or sprinkle? And then, will we immerse or sprinkle children? Where will we do these things? Indoors or out of doors? In still water or flowing water? How close will we choose to be to New Testament practices?

- For the Lord's Supper, what format shall we use? Shall we make it a Passover meal, thus ensuring that at least in its form we are as close as possible to the Last Supper? Even more basic, what shall we call this ritual? A Supper? A Communion? A Eucharist? A Mass? A proposal for change, once implemented, would paint the Army into one ritualistic corner or another.

- For any ritual we embrace or devise, what theology shall we attach to it? What will we tell the Salvationists of the world is the spiritual meaning and significance of it? What will we tell them is happening in the ritual that did not happen and was not available to us before we embraced the ritual?

- How will we measure worldwide whether or not the new rituals are curing the disease they are meant to cure? If they fail to cure it, would we re-adopt our prophetic witness to spiritual essentials, or would it be too late by then?

- How often should we hold whatever ritual (or rituals) are proposed? Even our architecture and internal design of halls and citadels would have to change to reflect our new-found reliance upon the usefulness and centrality of the rituals. I say 'centrality', for how could anything not regarded as central be allowed to be the ground of a claim that we are somehow discharged by God from our historical role to the other churches?

- Any serious proposal for change must also tell us what place these rituals will have or play in our key worship events apart from regular Sunday gatherings. Would there be divisional or territorial rituals, such as at Commissionings, public welcome meetings and the like? If not, why not? Would we see such rituals in our training colleges, in our officers' councils, in our local officers' seminars? What is it that would be happening in the future with the ritual that could not or does not happen now? Would participation be mandatory for officers? Would a divisional commander be required by his or her leaders to preside, to serve or otherwise to participate?

- This question leads to a bigger one that any proposal must address. What provision will the Army make for soldiers, local officers, or officers whose consciences will not allow them to be a part of whatever it is that is being proposed by way of change? Any proposal would need to demonstrate why these comrades would still be wanted as part of the new history-free but ritually-sensitive Army. For many the matter goes very deep indeed. A proposal for change must be sure to show that the consciences of such as these will not be ridden over roughshod.

- Any proposal will also have to tell us what we are to tell the other churches about our *volte-face*. Many of them do, in fact, truly respect and understand our present position. Dr Charles S. Duthie contributed a chapter to *Vocation and Victory* (Brunnen 1975) in which he wrote: 'I believe that the Church of Christ owes much to The Salvation Army for reminding us that our unity basically consists in our being "in Christ", and for showing us, by its practice, that we must urge men to enter decisively by God's grace into this condition.'

BAPTISM

A Statement on Baptism

After full and careful consideration of The Salvation Army's understanding of, and approach to, the sacrament of water baptism, the International Spiritual Life Commission sets out the following points regarding the relationship between a soldier's swearing-in and water baptism.

1 Only those who confess Jesus Christ as Saviour and Lord may be considered for soldiership in The Salvation Army.

2 Such a confession is confirmed by the gracious presence of God the Holy Spirit in the life of the believer and includes the call to discipleship.

3 In accepting the call to discipleship Salvationists promise to continue to be responsive to the Holy Spirit and to seek to grow in grace.

4 They also express publicly their desire to fulfil membership of Christ's Church on earth as soldiers of The Salvation Army.

5 The Salvation Army rejoices in the truth that all who are in Christ are baptised into the one body by the Holy Spirit (1 Corinthians 12:13).

6 It believes, in accordance with Scripture, that 'there is one body and one Spirit . . . one Lord, one faith, one baptism; one God and Father of all, who is over all and through all and in all' (Ephesians 4:5, 6).

7 The swearing-in of a soldier of The Salvation Army beneath the Trinitarian sign of the Army's flag acknowledges this truth.

8 It is a public response and witness to a life-changing encounter with Christ which has already taken place, as is the water baptism practised by some other Christians.

9 The Salvation Army acknowledges that there are many worthy ways of publicly witnessing to having been baptised into Christ's body by the Holy Spirit and expressing a desire to be his disciple.

10 The swearing-in of a soldier should be followed by a lifetime of continued obedient faith in Christ.

Notes on Baptism

(taken from 'The Sacraments according to St Paul and St John', a paper presented by Captain John Read)

If the word 'sacrament' has any kind of biblical root, then that root is to be found in Paul's writings. The English word 'sacrament' is a translation of the Latin *sacramentum* which appears in the Vulgate as a translation of the Greek *mysterion*.

Although the word appears once in the synoptic Gospels, and once in Revelation, Paul is the only writer to use it in a systematic way. In 1 Corinthians Paul writes about God's secret wisdom (2:7) which is the proclamation of the cross. 'Jesus Christ and him crucified' is the *mysterion* of God. Those who proclaim the apostolic message of God's intervention in history in the person and passion of Jesus Christ are 'stewards of the mysteries of God' (1 Corinthians 4:1 *AV*).

In each and every reference within the New Testament *mysterion* applies to the action of God, not of man. It is never applied to the action of the Church, and never to baptism or to the breaking of bread. In fact, there is no word which applies to these actions of initiation and incorporation within the Christian community and brings them together under a common heading. Paul certainly never uses *mysterion* in this way, or any other word instead.

The appellation of the Latin *sacramentum* to the rituals of baptism and Holy Communion indicates a shift in understanding as to the mystery which lies at the heart of the faith.

The shift ultimately gave the word 'sacrament' a meaning which did not derive from *mysterion* in its primitive and radical New Testament usage, but from the context of the mystery cults. As Karl Barth wrote it came to be that *'mysterion* = re-presentation of the cultic deity (by ritualistic means) = means of grace'.

The alternative to 'means of grace' (the 'Sacraments') is immediacy of grace, and for Paul one word is shorthand for this immediacy –

'Spirit'. Because of the Spirit we are filled with the resurrection life and power of Christ, we have the mind of Christ, we are being transformed from within.

If for Paul the one and only sacrament is Christ, then how did Paul understand baptism and the Lord's Supper? Both are mentioned in an intriguing passage in 1 Corinthians 10:1-4. Here Paul compares the forefathers of the Old Testament with the Church, the new Israel, and he talks about the forefathers being baptised into Moses in the cloud and the sea. The cloud was the pillar of cloud that they followed through the wilderness, the sea, the Red Sea which parted before them as they fled from the Egyptians. These people, Paul says, were marked out by two events: their 'baptism into Moses' and their sharing together in spiritual food and drink.

This brief passage by its comparisons confirms that this early Christian community was marked out by two events 'pregnant with meaning': baptism and the breaking of bread, and by one concept which bound the two together – the notion of the Church as the body of Christ.

'Baptised into Christ' is shorthand for 'baptised into the body of Christ' (confirmed in 1 Corinthians 12:13). Sacramental scholars argue that phrases such as 'baptised into Christ' and 'baptised into one body' are given such weight and significance within the total context of Paul's teaching that they 'imply (more than) a merely symbolical interpretation'.

However, this doesn't mean that we have to opt for a 'mystical', 'magical' or 'sacramental' interpretation because what these scholars fail to fully take into account is the strength, depth and consistency of Paul's understanding of the Church as the body of Christ. The Body was a reality for Paul not in the spiritual realm alone, but visibly and publicly. It is a social and spiritual reality. The body of Christ is a holistic reality for Paul.

Paul says of the old Israel 'they were all baptised into Moses in the cloud and the sea'.

'Into Moses' means:

● They became the people of Moses and the people of God.

● They went from the rule of Pharaoh to the rule of Moses and the rule of God.

● They went from captivity to freedom.

'Baptised' means:

- They followed.

- They were obedient and accepted the command and discipline of Moses.

- They acted in faith. They fled.

- They shared together in an unforgettable event which marked the passing from an old life into a new one, or from death to life.

We might choose to note that in this baptism none of them got wet.

In Romans (6:3, 4) Paul writes: 'Don't you know that all of us who are baptised into Christ Jesus were baptised into his death? We were therefore buried with him through baptism into death in order that, just as Christ was raised from the dead through the glory of the Father, we too may live a new life.'

This passage, more than any other, lies behind the quasi-sacramentalism of those modern evangelicals who insist that nothing less than total immersion will do. They are missing the point. It is not the plunging into the waters which matters but the entry 'into Christ', and the incorporation of the believer into 'the body of Christ'.

For the apostle Paul baptism and the breaking of bread are assumed to be the identifying and characteristic actions of the gathered community of faith. Baptism is the accepted means of incorporation into the body of Christ, the Lord's Supper, the accepted manner of participation.

However, neither of these is understood in any 'sacramental' sense, for Christ is the 'sacrament of God'. Paul does understand them 'holistically'. The spiritual cannot be separated from the material or the social in these matters.

There does not seem to be grounds here on which to object to an alternative cultural equivalent to baptism such as the swearing-in of soldiers. The requirement is for a public act of incorporation into the community, into the body. Effectively the swearing-in ceremony would seem to be a kind of 'dry baptism'. However, there are no grounds for absolutist assertions which would maintain, without question, the permanence within a movement of such an alternative.

The meal as described by Paul does not justify any sacramental interpretations or understandings of the Lord's Supper. But neither does it justify the discontinuation, or discouragement of, the meal.

In fact the command to remembrance would seem to have a permanent and absolute character, as also would Paul's teaching that the fellowship of Christians should be real and visible and not ideal and invisible.

This primitive and powerful form of Christianity is a challenge to most forms of church within the modern world.

The many references to baptisms and meals, to water and bread and wine all show that the Christian community out of which the Gospel of John emerged and for which the apostle wrote, practised baptism and the breaking of bread just like the churches in Jerusalem and Corinth and elsewhere.

However, in John's Gospel it is almost as if all overt references to the Christian practice of baptism and the breaking of bread have been carefully deleted. John does not give us any reason to suspect the truth of those gospel accounts which describe how Jesus was baptised by John, or that he spoke unforgettable and significant words at the final meal he shared with the disciples, but he gives us no record of them. Whatever we make of it there is a reason for these omissions.

Such references as there are to baptism and the breaking of bread seem to question rather than support these practices.

We have already noted that John does not record the baptism of Jesus by John although he records the encounter between the two. John is the one who baptises with water. Jesus is the one who baptises with the Holy Spirit (John 1:29-34).

The water which Jesus turned into wine at Cana had been intended for use in ceremonial washing, and baptism is later described by the evangelist as 'ceremonial washing' (John 3:25).

The reference to birth by water and Spirit in the conversation with Nicodemus (John 3:5) – 'I tell you the truth, no one can enter the Kingdom of God unless he is born of water and the Spirit' – is often held to refer to water baptism. Yet Jesus is talking here about two not three kinds of birth, and the simplest understanding would be that he is talking about natural birth and spiritual rebirth.

Jesus told the Samaritan woman of the gift of 'living water' – 'a spring of water welling up to eternal life'. John later explained that this living water is the gift of the Spirit (John 7:39).

John makes clear that the practice of baptism originated with the disciples and not with Jesus. He states explicitly that Jesus did not baptise (John 4:2). In so doing he raises the interesting question of who baptised the Twelve – or more – who baptised everyone else on the day of Pentecost, and their status or standing in Christ.

From all of this it seems most probable that John is writing in a situation where baptism and the breaking of bread are beginning to take on a 'sacramental' significance. In opposition and response to this, John commandeers every sign and every symbol in order to underline the truth that Jesus is the Word made flesh, and that it is by means of the Incarnation that God has acted in space and time to make his grace and presence known in the Son.

If we ask, 'By what means are the grace and presence of God mediated to mankind when the Son has ascended to the Father?' the answer according to John is, 'By means of the *Paracletos* – the Comforter, the Holy Spirit.' In John's Gospel, water, bread and wine are signs pointing to the only sacrament, the Word made flesh, to the Holy Spirit and to a humanity recreated by Word and Spirit.

If we are tempted to allow our preconceptions, our prejudices to temper our response to this, then maybe we should for a final moment consider the manner and the means of the shattering of some first-century Jewish world views.

In 1 Corinthians 8:6 Paul wrote: 'For us there is but one God, the Father, from whom all things came and for whom we live; and there is but one Lord, Jesus Christ, through whom all things came and for whom we live.' Here Paul's experience of the living reality of Christ in the Spirit leads him to shatter the most sacred Jewish text, the Shemah, recited from childhood: 'Hear, O Israel: The Lord our God, the Lord is one' (Deuteronomy 6:4).

John places on the lips of Thomas the highest claim of his Gospel regarding the person of our Lord Jesus. To the living, crucified man, Thomas declared: 'My Lord and my God.'

This is sacrament, this is mystery and this is immediacy. 'God with us.' Immanuel.

William Booth on the Sacraments

112

William Booth on the Sacraments
(from 'The General's New Year address to officers'– The War Cry *17 January 1883*)

Talking about churches leads me to another question, which I know is of some interest to all of you, and to many others – viz, the Sacraments.

Here we will make a statement which will help to dismiss any serious anxiety from your minds very considerably, I have no doubt, as it has done with us, and this is one in which I think you will all agree.

The Sacraments must not, nay, they cannot, rightly be regarded as conditions of salvation. If you make them essentials, if you say that men cannot get to Heaven without being baptised with water, or without 'breaking bread', as it is called, where there is the opportunity of doing so, then you shut out from that holy place a multitude of men and women who have been and are today sincere followers of the Lord Jesus Christ, who honestly believe his words and earnestly strive to keep them. This would be a very great calamity, and I cannot accept it for a moment.

I think you will perceive that any order from me for the general administration of the Sacraments would be likely to produce grave dissensions. There is a very great and widespread difference of opinion with regard to the modes of administration – one half of the religious world denying in toto the efficacy of the Sacraments as administered by the other half. Our Baptist friends, for instance, contend that baptism as administered to infants by the Church of England, Methodists, and others, is no baptism at all, and when we gave consent for some of our people to take part in the Church of England sacrament, the clergyman who invited them seized the opportunity for showing them that they were only in part qualified to receive the ordinance, seeing that part had been confirmed, and a part not. Another gentleman of very high position recommended that that part of our people who had not been confirmed should go to the dissenters for the ordinance, while the portion who had been confirmed should go to the

113

church. This you will see would have divided us at the very door of the church. Here would have been a very great difficulty at once.

Now if the Sacraments are not conditions of salvation, if there is a general division of opinion as to the proper mode of administering them, and if the introduction of them would create division of opinion and heart-burning, and if we are not professing to be a church, nor aiming at being one, but simply a force for aggressive salvation purposes, is it not wise for us to postpone any settlement of the question, to leave it over to some future day, when we shall have more light, and see more clearly our way before us?

Meanwhile, we do not prohibit our own people in any shape or form from taking the Sacraments. We say, 'If this is a matter of your conscience, by all means break bread.' The churches and chapels all round about will welcome you for this, *but in our own ranks let us be united,* and go on our way, and mind our own business. Let us remember him who died for us continually. Let us remember his love every hour of our lives, and continually feed on him – not on Sundays only, and then forget him all the week, but let us by faith eat his flesh and drink his blood continually; and 'whatsoever you do, whether you eat or drink, do all to the glory of God'.

And further, there is one baptism on which we are all agreed – the one baptism of the Bible – that is the baptism of the Holy Ghost, of which baptism John spoke as vastly superior and more important than the baptism of water, when he said, 'I indeed baptise you with water, but One cometh after me whose shoe's latchet I am not worthy to unloose; he shall baptise you with the Holy Ghost and with fire.'

Be sure you insist upon that baptism. Be sure you enjoy that baptism yourselves, and be sure you insist upon it for your people, not only for the adults but for the children.

We are bringing out a formal service for the dedication of children. It will be put into your hands in a few days. By this soldiers can introduce their children to the Army. Before this dedicatory service is gone through, you must explain it to the parents, and show them that unless they are willing to bring up their children as soldiers and officers in the Army, they cannot have any part in it.

Let us keep off mere forms and do nothing in which, as far as possible, the hearts of our soldiers do not go with us.

The International Spiritual Life Commission Membership

The International Spiritual Life Commission was formed by General Paul A. Rader to examine and emphasise those things which are at the heart of The Salvation Army. The membership, listed below, was made up of officers and non-officers, who came from different countries, representing various areas of Army service.

The deliberations were marked by an understanding of the varied needs and hopes of different territories and cultures, and took place in a spirit of unity, for which all members give thanks.

The following officers and soldiers were appointed to serve as members of the International Spiritual Life Commission. Ranks given are as they applied at the time:

Lieut-Colonel Robert Street (Chairman), Lieut-Colonel Earl Robinson (Secretary), Lieut-Colonel Linda Bond, Captain Teofilo Chagas, Commissioner Doreen Edwards, Dr Roger Green, Lieut-Colonel Margaret Hay, Sister Susan Harris, CSM Warren Johnson, Lieut-Colonel David Lofgren, Colonel Emmanuel Miaglia, Lieut-Colonel Stuart Mungate, Colonel Phil Needham, Major Lyell Rader, Captain John Read, Captain Oscar Sanchez and Major N.M. Vijayalakshmi.

Corresponding members who also attended some of the Commission's deliberations were:

Commissioner Ian Cutmore (former Chairman), Colonel Shaw Clifton, Major Ian Barr and Envoy William van Graan.

Other corresponding members who assisted:

Lieut-Colonel David Kim, Chong-won, Colonel Douglas Davis, Commissioner Peter Chang and Recruiting Sergeant John Bayliss.

The Commission met for five separate weeks.